SAY YES

TO

SAYING NO

SAY YES

TO

SAYING NO

Set Your Boundaries
For Success

Leslie Fierling

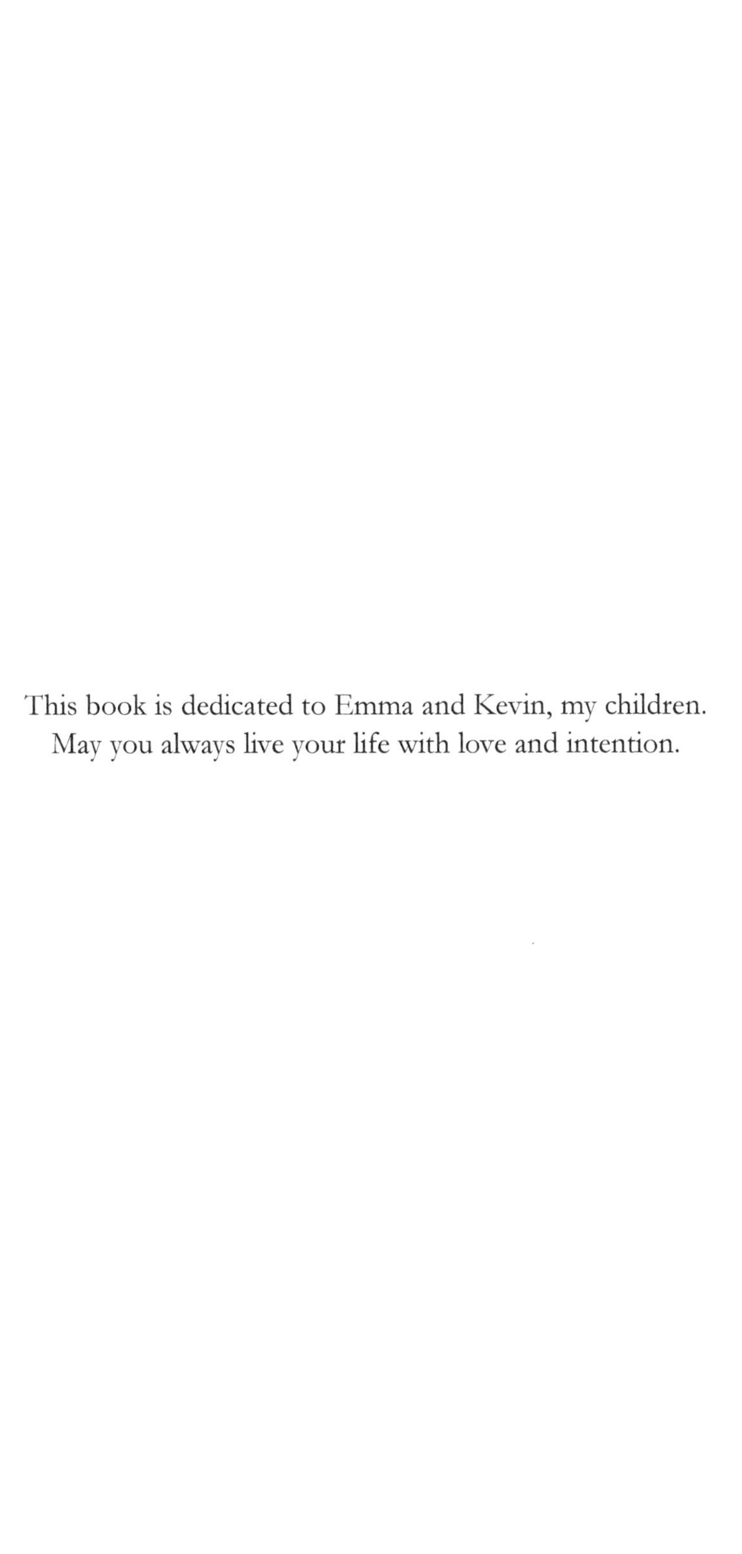
This book is dedicated to Emma and Kevin, my children.
May you always live your life with love and intention.

Acknowledgements

Kevin and Emma, my children, who have been supportive and helpful in my journey of life and in the writing of this book. Erv and Dorothy Kuch, my caring parents, who have always been there for me and inspired me to chase my dreams. Fred Fierling, my ex-husband, who taught me so much about business and being an entrepreneur.

Julie Salisbury, my publisher, who has been inspirational while exhibiting integrity and "walks the talk". Thank you Julie for showing me how to write and get my message out into the world in the form of a published book. And alongside, a big thank you to Greg Salisbury for his patience and many roles in the creation of this book. The gift of an insightful editor is priceless; therefore, I extend my thanks to Kendra Langeteig for your patience and hard work and to Janet Love Morrison for proof reading.

Many of my dearest friends have listened to me, debated with me, and been patient with me throughout the journey of this book. Thank you Helen McDonald, Claudette McDowell, Doug Rose, and Joan Skoye.,. I am grateful for so many friends and acquaintances who are willing to connect wherever they can: Jim Rennie who goes the extra mile to help out (and is an incredible cook); Dave McKee who volunteers for our ski club and always brings a smile to my face; and Leslie Wagner-Fierling who was the best sister-in-law a girl could have.

In closing, one final acknowledgement to my daughter Emma: her commitment and contribution to my dream has been immeasurable. She is the graphic designer for my website, my branding, my business, and so much more.

Contents

Preface
The Wake-Up Call - Discovering My Boundaries

Sometimes it takes a crisis to force us to see who we really are and what's most important to us in life. My big wake up call hit me like a kick in the heart with a series of three life crises. After years of running a successful business, my husband and I found ourselves in the eleventh hour of a bankruptcy journey. A few years later, I was diagnosed with breast cancer. After surviving this crisis, we struggled to face the reality that our marriage of twenty-three years was on the brink of collapse. I hope it doesn't take a life crisis for you to get clarity about yourself and what you want, but that's what it took for me. Like it or not, I was forced to take a long hard look at myself. Why did everything start spiralling completely out of control? To answer that question, I had to reflect more deeply on the way I was living my life. I knew it would involve more than making simple lifestyle changes to get healthy again.

What I learned came down to this: I wasn't being true to myself and I hadn't been for years. I was living a lie. The anguish of that self-betrayal impacted my health on every level. Deep down, I knew that I hadn't been listening to the cues from my body telling me that things weren't right. The stress in response of taking on too much work and compromising myself to meet the demands of a dysfunctional marriage had taken its toll on my health.

I'm one of the lucky ones. Those three wake-up calls gave me a chance to fix my life. The business recovered, I survived breast cancer, and I did everything in my power to save my marriage before it came to an end. One of the greatest lessons I learned from those difficult times was the importance of setting successful boundaries for myself. By successful, I mean boundaries that honour and reflect who you really are: your core values, beliefs, and aspirations. Boundaries that let you live by intention and choice, not according to what someone else thinks you should do. That's living by default. It is only by setting boundaries that you will be able to create a healthy balance in your relationships and in your professional life.

I invite you to read this book and reflect on your own life journey as I share insights, stories, and information to help you set supportive boundaries for yourself. The book begins with the topic of "experts" and shows how to set boundaries around all that information to make it work for you. Then we'll look at ways to get clarity for setting boundaries in your personal relationships and lifestyle choices, including diet and exercise. The second part of the book moves from the personal sphere into the workplace. We'll look at ways to set effective boundaries that support your personal and professional growth, whether you're an entrepreneur or an employee. The final chapter moves into the wider global community. You'll see how resourceful people with vision and integrity have crossed personal and geographic boundaries to contribute to the well being of others.

The real-life stories and information that I share with you are designed to help you take a stand on what you believe. I have strong opinions that I speak out on in this book. That's my passion – as well as my job – as a public speaker and workshop facilitator. I've been committed to helping people take control of their lives and reach their highest potential for many years in my consulting business. But I am not trying to convince you that my way of thinking is the right way for you. When it comes to setting boundaries in our lives, there's no absolute right way to go about it, no one-size-fits-all template for you to be successful in everything you do. But I think there's one point we will agree on: to be happy in life, you have to be true to yourself. I spent years not being true to myself by living a life that didn't work for me. I can't get those years back. They're gone. That loss encouraged me to live in a way that enhances my growth and brings me great fulfillment. I wish the same for you: a life fulfilled and your growth continually enhanced. I hope this book will inspire you to wake up, take charge, and set boundaries to create the life you want!

Chapter 1
Are You Giving Away Your Power?
Be Your Own Best Expert

There are no facts, only interpretations.
Friedrich Nietzsche

Let's begin thinking about boundaries by looking at the "experts" in your life. There are thousands of experts out there ready to give you advice on almost anything imaginable. Their advice and opinions can influence what you think and challenge the boundaries you have about certain things. If you're not careful, an expert can erode or destroy some of the boundaries in your life that are actually healthy ones. On the other hand, a credible expert can offer information and guidance to help you set boundaries that are smart, respectful, strong and really support who you are and what you want in life.

As you read about the experts in this chapter, remember the most important lesson:

Don't give away your power.

With the overwhelming amount of information available, where do you turn when you need some professional advice to make an important decision? Let's say you want to find out how to deal with a health issue or start your own business. Like most people, I only have so much time in a day to do the research. I can't become an expert in everything that's important to me. So I look for an experienced professional – an expert. The problem is, how do you know what to believe when there are so many experts and opinions out there? The Canadian Broadcast Company (CBC) documentary, "The Trouble with Experts," written and directed by Josh Freed, makes the case that the "cult of the experts" has virtually become a new religion with all the answers to help guide us in our lives. Freed shows that, often times, experts don't actually have the knowledge that they claim. As a matter of fact, the information we get can be blatantly wrong and our own guesses could be just as valid.

There is hardly any area of our lives where we don't see the influence of the new "cult of experts": diets, nutrition, cures for cancer, diseases, spirituality, self-help, exercise trends, corporate culture, financial management, wine connoisseurship, art buying, family and relationship counseling – the list goes on. The "cult of experts" is making a lot of money from gullible consumers buying into their so-called "expertise". The financial gurus that encouraged people to invest in real estate had no clue about the financial crisis of 2008.

There is a mindset at play that makes us susceptible to listening to the "expert's" advice. Because there is so much information out there, we're desperate for anyone to lead us down the right path. We want someone to know the answers. We love gurus of science, religion, the government, and the economy because these "experts" all claim to know the answers and give us the certainty we are longing for. The harsh reality is that there are many things that we can't be certain about and for which no one has the "right" answer. William White, a retired senior bank executive, explains that we are like "the little child that always wants to believe that somebody's in charge. There isn't anyone in charge." He goes on to say, "We want to believe that someone knows and someone really understands because the alternative to confront all of this, what is essentially chaos, is very difficult for people to live with" ("The Trouble with Experts" CBC). The "experts" rely on that insecurity to get you to relinquish your own opinions or questions.

When you're presented with information on a subject that's new and unfamiliar, especially if it has a lot of scientific "facts," this information can be intimidating. So you call in the expert. The question is, if you choose to believe a so-called expert and "buy" the program and/or products being pitched, who is benefitting? Let's take a closer look to help you to answer that question.

What's Wrong with this Picture?

Would you take advice from a financial advisor who is flat broke or just making ends meet? Do not be fooled into thinking that someone is financially successful just because that person happens to drive a fancy car or look rich. Would you take medical advice from someone who doesn't have a medical license to practice? Look for the certificates nailed on the office wall. Would you have confidence in a marriage counselor who has been married and divorced several times? Don't be fooled by appearances. How can you tell the real expert from the fake expert?

"Fake it 'til you make it"
Consulting & Coaching in Business

Consulting and coaching in the business world is an area of so-called expertise that seriously concerns me. There is an overabundance of "coaches" in the market who lack valid experience and education. Consultant Matthew Stewart, author of *The Management Myth*, shares his story of having only three weeks of training before being sent out to work for a management-consulting firm as an "expert." His clients bought into his expertise without doing any research into his background qualifications.

Experience Counts

If you're thinking about hiring a business coach for your company, take a good look into that person's background. Has the expert coach experienced firsthand the problems you are having? When, where, how long? Are you paying outrageous fees for mere common sense? Are you paying for someone to ask you questions that you could ask yourself? How can a person with virtually no coaching experience on his resume, or someone who takes basic common sense and blows it up into great new wisdom be a credible coach? Credibility comes with serious education along with real-life experience. Why would an entrepreneur or CEO pay for a coach who has never owned a business of substantial size and taken personal financial risk? Without such background, any consulting advice is "fluffy" and someone's intellectual guesses, at best. If it were your business and financial investments at stake, wouldn't you want a coach or consultant with solid experience?

"But I'm worth it."

When hiring a consultant or coach, I suggest looking carefully at fees, along with experience and education. Too many times the cost of an "expert opinion" is seriously overpriced. We have gone over the top in our business culture with the concept of "I'm worth it". Trainers and coaches have that attitude and clients are attracted to their expensive programs because they too are worth it. It's a two-way marketing ploy. There needs to be a "correction in the market," or should I say, a correction in some overly puffed up egos. Where is the balance? Some of the fees that are asked by business coaches are outrageous for what you get. If a CEO needs some coaching in certain areas, that person should take time to do the research and find support from a specialist.

During my training as a presenter and speaker, I was disappointed by an experience with a business coach who started our coaching session with the "mirroring" method. This is a method where your questions are repeated (mirrored) back to you and then you answer the question yourself. This may work for some, but for me it felt like an insult to my intelligence. I can talk to myself at home for free instead of paying a $500 per hour fee. When you hire someone, make sure your background check is thorough. On the positive side, I can say that I have worked with business consultants who met high standards and I was satisfied with their level of expertise. There are consultants and coaches who do deserve our respect and admiration.

The strategy of "faking it" may work if you're trying to change your mood, but it does not hold credibility when becoming an expert, or at least it shouldn't. Faking expertise and not being truly qualified is not good enough for me to believe someone else's advice. Is it for you? How quickly do you believe what you hear without checking out the credentials of the person claiming to be an expert? I encourage you to take the time to do your research on any expert before giving away your money and power. And don't forget to check out if the expert "walks the talk".

Wannabe Experts School

Did you know there are "expert schools" that teach you how to sell yourself as the expert? For a few days of training, expect to pay between $2000 and $7000. You will get media training as well as lessons for learning to use the right jargon to sound like a true expert. You will learn how to present yourself to the world as "the expert".

Get the Buzz Going

Another tip for new experts is to get visibility in the media, especially TV. The TV networks like to feature experts in heated discussions for cheap entertainment value. What a great way to get quoted! Getting quoted is exactly what the upcoming expert needs and wants. Whether the statement is true or not doesn't matter. The more outrageous, the more it attracts attention.

How to Look the Part

Matthew Stewart, the author of *The Management Myth, Why the Experts Keep Getting It Wrong*, gives tips on how to "look the part" and establish authority. He says, "Be tall, show signs of wealth, wear expensive clothes, jewellry, drive expensive cars, stay in the high end hotels, master the jargon … nothing sells like success … to establish your expertise. You demonstrate your expertise with your result." Don't be fooled by appearances. The expert you see on stage or in the ad may be grossly in debt for keeping up a false display of wealth.

The Management Guru

Along with the rise in business coaches and consultants, there is a near epidemic of management gurus on the market. According to Matthew Stewart, in his interview with CBC "The whole field of management is a dressed up façade that pretends business is a science run on formulas. This is unfounded. There are no genuine experts"("Trust Me, I Am an Expert" CBC Doc Zone). Stewart goes on to explain that math formulas cannot be used in an environment with unpredictable human behavior. He states, "Formulas, studies, science - all that sounds so factual and absolute." What I also see and object to is the word "science" being abused and overused. The general public will assume information is factual when the word "science" is attached. Usually the word "studies" is included with the "scientific" information.

If you look at how certain studies are conducted, you'd see how results are made to happen. You could start with the result you want and build a "study" around it that would produce that outcome. For example, let's imagine you want the study to show that a positive work environment increases sales for the company. You could provide the employees with presentations every morning that boosted positive thinking and morale. Let's say sales went up since you implemented this program. Are you sure it was the positive thinking that increased sales? Or was it the nutritious breakfast and or caffeine served at these meetings that gave the perception of more positive energy? Or was it the increased need in the economy for your widgets? Or was it the increased advertising campaign that influenced more buyers? This is an oversimplified example, but the point remains. Most studies are shaded and do not consider all possibilities since the needed outcome is predetermined and usually because there is money to be made.

Fact or Fiction?
The Illusion of "Knowledge"

In his book, *WRONG, Why Experts Keep Failing Us – And How to Know When Not to Trust Them*, David Freedman claims, "On average, two thirds of studies in the top medical journals, which are written by respected academic experts, are wrong." He goes on to say, "Virtually all of the studies published in economics journals are wrong."

The more research I did into the questionable accuracy of information used by experts, the more statistics I found confirming huge rates of incompetency. Author Ben Goldacre shows us that for years, huge amounts of negative data have gone missing and this is still the norm. This leaves well-intended doctors prescribing drugs to people based on mostly false or missing information (Goldacre, *Bad Science*).

How do we get hooked into blindly accepting what someone tells us to be the "facts"? One or two truths may be included in information with a host of other ideas that turn out to be absolutely absurd and false. People will buy into the whole package, believing it must **all** be true just because there is ten percent truth. Fad diets are an example of this kind of deception. I usually find a few true, confirmed and or proven facts dispersed throughout a fad diet book. This strategy can be used for any subject, from health to science or religion.

I would look carefully at the pseudoscience surrounding any new theories on any subject. Using sophisticated vocabulary that could intimidate the audience is often used to present information as facts when in reality the information is not factual at all.

Absolute Truth?

The information that an expert has to offer may work or be true for that person, but that does not mean it will work for you. Maybe it will. It depends if you share the same brain type, blood type, body chemistry, or similar environmental influences. There are some similarities, since we are all humans, when it comes to food, exercise, and medical issues. The commonality ends there and our uniqueness takes over. What works for me does not necessarily mean it will work for you.

There are no absolute truths, no perfect formulas. The problem is that we inhale information and are gullible enough to assume it must all be true. We want answers to questions and are desperate for someone to give them to us. It is much easier to believe an "authority" on the subject. So many of our questions and problems do not have black and white answers. Many times there is no absolute right or wrong way to do something. That is why people get stuck in a space and have trouble moving forward. Then it becomes so easy to listen to someone else's advice regardless of whether or not it is best for you.

So what do we do about this? The best solution is to be diligent about doing your research on the experts and their studies. Start with the experts. Look into their backgrounds. Are they really graduates from a prestigious college? If they got their doctor's degree from a university you do not recognize, google it. Do you see credentials that required nothing more than a payment for the piece of paper that says someone has a "degree"? Is the "expert" actually a doctor in the field of expertise? Does the expert's point of view make sense? Or are their theories and explanations based on "opinion"? How easy is it to see another point of view and be just as correct?

Do your best to be aware of all the problems and misleading information in studies and research. Then decide what you will adopt - or not. Do not take information from a study as the absolute truth. Consider it but know there are flaws in any study. Educate yourself as much as possible from different sources. For example, when I considered what to do with my breast cancer treatment, I wanted to know about all my options in modern medicine as well as the options from naturopathic doctors.

Although many people have already wised up to become savvy consumers, many still have not. It is time for the public to draw a line and set a boundary that says, "No more! We will not believe everything we are told, especially by the media. We will think for ourselves before giving away our money and power. We demand more truth. We demand better research and more diligent studies. We want to know how and when studies were conducted."

Make Sound Decisions First – then Act

It has been said, over and over again, that doing something is better than doing nothing. I agree that being frozen and unable to do anything is not a good place to be. Yet, there are times when **doing nothing is the best course of action**. Sometimes we need that time to process the information or wait for circumstances to present themselves that give us the information we need to make a well thought out decision. Only you know when it's time to draw the line and say enough waiting or enough gathering information and move on.

You can begin to set boundaries by targeting areas of expertise that look suspicious to you. Here are some examples of red flags for me in the "expert" business:

1. The Relationship Guru. Gurus that give advice on martial relationships but cannot succeed at their own. I have witnessed a couple that gave advice and workshops on having a great marriage yet behind the public scene, the husband was

having a multitude of affairs. What hypocrisy! No, I will not buy the guru's books, tickets for presentations, or anything else that supports this dishonourable career. If you do some of your own snooping around, you will find countless well-known "authorities" that have earned the label of hypocrite. If what they preach doesn't even work for themselves, who will it work for? How do you feel about taking advice on honesty and integrity from an authority that lies and plays dishonest games? Do you believe experts should practice what they preach?

2. The Financial Expert. All you have to do is look at the authorities in this field and ask their clients how they feel about the advice. Not only do we turn our personal power over to the gurus but we also hand over our hard earned money far too quickly. Is your financial advisor wealthy? No? Then how will that person help you become wealthy? Or are you just contributing to your advisor's wealth? Do diligent research before buying into any kind of financial plan. After that, I highly recommend having a financial plan and using an advisor who meets your criteria.

3. The Sex Expert. Can anyone really tell you how to improve your sex life? It's wise to share ideas, wisdom, and seek education on the subject of sex, especially when things aren't working for you in this department. Getting physical and or medical help, such as addressing hormonal issues with estrogen and testosterone, or getting emotional support in understanding yourself or others is highly recommended. Do everything you can to know yourself. Then and only then, will you be able to decipher what is valid for you in the advice you hear. One kind of authority that does not work for me is a man who claims to be an expert on "how to turn a woman on" sexually. If you want to understand some general techniques on the subject, ask a woman not a man. Then (gentlemen) ask the individual woman you are having

sex with to tell you what really works for her. We, men and women, have our unique gender characteristics. On top of that, we each are unique individuals, whether we are talking about our sexuality or any other aspect of ourselves. Educate your partner rather than leave it up to him or her to seek information from others that are truly not experts about you.

4. The Wine Expert. Don't Be Fooled by Labels. The CBC documentary, "The Trouble With Experts" states, "Most wine experts can't tell a great wine from an ordinary one". Taste tests were done using the same wine in two different bottles. One bottle had a cheap label and one bottle had an expensive label. Over fifty percent of the experts preferred the wine in the bottle with the expensive label. Also, blind taste testing was done switching wine from a $30 bottle with the wine from a $500 bottle. The majority of experts still chose the wine from the $500 bottle, without knowing it contained the $30 wine. Any bottle of wine costs only about $20 to produce. The high cost of the expensive wines is due to mythology and marketing.

The bottom line here is to choose the wine that tastes best to you. Our taste buds and perceptions are unique to each of us. I have experienced tasting wines from all over the world and have visited wineries in the United States, Europe, and Canada. Yet my favourite wines are produced by a British Columbian winery. Is this because it's close to home? Tastes are very subjective. Forget about fancy labels or "expert" opinions. When it comes to taste, your opinion is all that matters.

Here's to Your Health!

The health and wellness industry is overflowing with advice and information from self-proclaimed "experts," someone who has no real education, formal or otherwise and no relevant experience in the field. Yet these people speak as if they are absolute authorities on their subject, using words like "never," "always," "must," and "guarantee" to sell their product or service. Though I find examples of self-proclaimed experts everywhere, in every field, the health field is loaded. I met a man who wrote a book about nutrition. He didn't have a university education on the subject and he bought into whatever ideas he liked on the Internet, regardless of whether or not it was backed up by real science. Then, he preached his opinions as if they were the absolute truth for all mankind. If I followed his nutrition program, I would weigh 60 pounds more and never have the energy to perform in my recreational activities. Would you take nutritional advice from a celebrity? Look at all the celebrities who have written books on health issues and diets. They use their fame to sell books, which may have a few known truths at best, to create credibility. The rest of the information is based on hearsay, wishful thinking, or examples of what worked for them as individuals. This does not mean the approach will be good for you. In fact, it may be damaging to your health.

Dietary Supplements that Don't Add Up - for the Consumer

The word on the street is out: Our food sources are depleted of nutrients and our bodies are challenged by the stress of our environment. The experts say it's not enough to simply eat food any more. You have to add supplements to your diet. True?

Look at the studies on nutrients and supplements. Who is funding the studies that produce results that tell us we need "x" ml of "y" nutrient? We spend so much money on supplements in spite of the fact that there's little conclusive evidence to confirm that they're really beneficial. Often, we really have no idea whether or not they are needed or even good for us. Richard Beliveau, Ph.D and Denis Gingras, Ph.D., authors of *Foods That Fight Cancer, Preventing Cancer Through Diet*, make a case for why supplements do more harm than good. That's not a prevalent opinion in a society where millions of businesses are making millions of dollars producing and selling supplements. Here is where more extensive studies need to be done concerning the placebo effect. This opens a whole other world of possibilities. Who will be next to jump on this bandwagon with some marketing ideas to make money? Certainly not every nutrition guru is full of false information and a sneaky marketing scheme to get rich, but I recommend doing your research before believing any information.

Follow Your Own Best Hunch

When it comes to finding a health and or nutrition program that really works, there is no one way that works for everyone. Some people will thrive as vegans. Some people will thrive as carnivores. Some people need extra carbohydrates, or protein or fat, depending on their lifestyle, exercise routine, and individual chemical and hormonal make up. I immediately dismiss any author who states that his or her way of eating is the only way for everyone and there are studies and evidence to prove it. "Studies" and "evidence" are so shaded and biased. Again, look at who did the study and who is going to benefit financially from the study. Evidence? Really? Giving historical examples is not real evidence. "Cave men ate this way and never died of cancer!" No kidding! They didn't live long enough to get cancer. Many were eaten by tigers, lions, and bears. There is no way we can extrapolate what went on in people's bodies and lives "X" number of years ago. We can't even figure that out in our present time and place, let alone centuries ago.

When I was immersed in my research on diets to prevent and or heal from cancer, I found all the contradictory information frustrating and confusing to say the least. One trivial example was this. One book said never eat chocolate. Another book said to eat 40 grams of seventy percent organic coco everyday. Each point of view had a long "scientific" explanation. We will all decide which stance to take based on how we feel and our background. In the end, no one knows what is right for you. In the end, you may not know what is right for you. Take the course of action you feel is your best option and is most appealing based on your intuition and your intelligence.

When consulting anyone about your nutritional needs, make sure to look into the person's background. Does this person have a real degree from a real university? Is this degree in the area of nutrition or something else? If an author has M.D. beside his or her name, does that necessarily qualify this doctor to give nutritional advice? Maybe the doctor's degree is in medicine or psychology. Unqualified nutritionists give the real ones a bad name.

My Story
Lost in the Sea of "Experts" & Where to Turn?

There was a knock on the door and to my surprise it was my neighbour from down the street. Before I could ask her in, she blurted out that she was diagnosed with breast cancer. After some tears and hugs we got down to the business of what to do. She told me about all the due diligence she was doing to find out the best course of treatment. The conflicting and incomplete information was overwhelming. One doctor said this; another said that. The naturopathic doctor recommended something entirely different. Try reading all the medical information when you do not have a doctor's knowledge of all the terminology. It's overwhelming. I felt really sorry for her and grateful I was not in her shoes. To have to make any kind of decision about one's course of action when dealing with cancer is a guessing game at best. My neighbour did choose to have a mastectomy in the end. After several surgeries for the disease and reconstruction she finally got through it and started living her life again.

Two years later I was the one knocking on her door. We were both so angry that we were the ones who lived all the "right, healthy" lifestyle choices to avoid this and still were diagnosed with breast cancer. So began my journey with the conflicting information from the "experts," only to again find out, through my personal experience, that there are no experts. No one knows what is right for you. So what did I do? Like my friend, I visited more than one doctor and asked a lot of questions. I bought a ton of books on the subject and had my husband help me read through them. He was much more able to read, decipher, and understand the information than I was. I was in an emotional state of shock and decisions had to be made quickly. I was grateful for his ability to read through and interpret the information. I ended up consenting to surgery to remove the lump and another one to remove lymph nodes and clean out the margins. I had radiation treatment, no chemotherapy and was on tamoxifen for four years and four months.

That being said, my greatest insight into the world of experts was through my breast cancer support group. There were about twenty of us. Women from all religious, economic, and educational backgrounds shared their emotional and medical journeys. One "doctor" prescribed a couple of thousand dollars worth of Chinese herbs for one woman. My Chinese acupuncturist who had been working with cancer patients for over thirty years told me never to take herbs of any kind, for he felt they lowered the immune system and allowed the cancer to grow faster. He recommended using the money I would spend on herbs to buy a new dress and a fun vacation. Lower the stress and have more fun in life was his best advice along with prescribing the acupuncture. He also supported all the modern medical treatments we have now even though they have their downfalls. Nothing is absolutely guaranteed.

Some went down the path of strictly listening to their naturopathic doctors. Some took the modern road. Some tried fad courses of treatment. Some lived. Some died. What course of treatment they believed in made no difference to their longevity:

but that's my opinion. The only real input that would be of real use would be from a cancer cell that could communicate to us. That is not possible at this point in time. So where does that leave us with regards to experts? I feel there are people in this field who are truly doing their best to find answers. The truth is that we have not yet found the answers. So each individual has to gather information as thoroughly as possible, decipher it to the best of their knowledge and make a decision. The experiences of another's journey in the world of cancer may or may not shed light on what you should do. Yet I highly recommend comparing as many stories as possible as well as getting your modern tests done. When you do decide to believe one expert or another, ask yourself what is motivating you to believe this person over another. Is it the fear in you the expert is addressing? Does the information or advice make sense to your set of beliefs and values? Is the cost going to leave you in poverty if you live? Mostly, you have to rely on yourself to read, listen, learn, and then go with your best instinct.

There are many debates between the benefits of modern medical practices versus the new "natural" medical approach to health care and healing. One hot issue is the debate between mammograms and thermography (a way of looking at breast tissue without radiation). I have experienced both procedures. It was the mammogram though that caught my breast cancer early and saved my life. I am aware of the inadequacies and down side of mammograms, but they do accomplish the goal of detecting breast cancer more often than not. No test is absolutely perfect. No breast tissue will look exactly the same in any test.

Ultimately each person needs to decide for herself what she feels comfortable doing. What I object to, as a breast cancer survivor, is the notion that only one way is the best way. When it comes to managing my own health, I choose to seek answers from both realms. What gave me the most clarity was asking myself what course of treatment gave me the best odds for living long enough to finish raising my children. The answer was clear for me. It was the modern medicine. I could not experiment with new ideas or theories or fad cures when it came to my children's best interests. They needed me alive.

Even researching in both fields of medicine, there are many things that we humans still don't know and have not discovered. There are no absolute answers at this point in time. The biggest boundary I recommend for you to set: Don't allow yourself to be gullible.

Beware of "The Power of Positive Thinking"

When I was finished with my radiation treatment for breast cancer, I attended a two-day workshop exclusive to cancer patient survivors. One of the speakers talked about a study done on survivors who did all the right things: eating nutritiously; exercising; avoiding alcohol, drugs and smoking; keeping low stress levels; finding love in their lives; and maintaining a positive attitude about conquering cancer and living a long life. These case studies were complied in a book about 13 cm (five inches) thick. The point was to "prove," with the impressive number of case studies in this huge book, how positive thinking can keep cancer away. Two issues came up for me. First of all, to make the conclusion that it was positive thinking rather than something else, such as lifestyle or stress reduction that outsmarted the cancer, was an outrageous assumption, a conclusion based mostly on fantasy. And what if the case studies of all the people that did the exact same things and still died of cancer were put into a book? That book would be much thicker. No mention of the latter was made. When I asked about those who died anyway, my question was brushed aside. I was told that if the cancer came back it was my fault for not having the right mental attitude and believing that "mind over matter" would conquer all. The positive thinking gurus make it sound as though it's our fault we get cancer, that there's something wrong in our thoughts that prevents us from healing. There is no real evidence that optimism adds time to one's life. Although I would certainly agree that being positive and happy makes for a more pleasant and enjoyable life with less stress.

It seems shameful that the positive thinking culture makes people feel guilty for things truly beyond their control. To say that someone can bring misfortune into their life because of their thoughts is wrong. Millions of positive thinkers are genetically predisposed to diseases such as cancer, MS, Parkinson's, or Huntington's. Must they live with guilt because they didn't know how to think the "right" way? How wrong to mislead them into thinking their ill health was their own fault because of their mental attitude. Or that they failed to cure themselves with positive thoughts. What about all those positive thinkers who smoke and still die of lung cancer? I am a great example of this. All my life I lived a healthy lifestyle with nutritional eating, exercise, and positive thinking. I believed I would die at the age of 92. I would never get cancer. Yet at 50, I had breast cancer. You could argue the fact that I had a lot of stress in my life that caused physical changes in my body, but shouldn't my positive thinking have had the power to negate all that bad stress and those imbalanced hormones?

The power of positive thinking gurus has also had a huge influence on people when it comes to their financial wellbeing. With the law of attraction, you can draw wealth and abundance to you by thinking and feeling rich. Many people who believed they could, would, and should be wealthy took foolish risks and gambled with important decisions to make it happen. Some of those positive thinkers became financially desperate with the economic downturn and found themselves homeless. As Barbara Ehrenreich states in *Bright-Sided: How Positive Thinking Is Undermining America,* "But the universe refused to play its assigned role as a 'big mail order department'. In complete defiance of the 'law of attraction,' long propounded by the gurus of positive thinking, things were getting worse for most Americans, not better."The media will report on any study, valid or not, that promotes the power of positive thinking. This sells. The media seems to grossly neglect studies that show no difference to longevity with a positive mental attitude. You may find these studies with some digging though.

This brings me around to the question of realism and where to draw the line. By giving so much credit to the power of positive thinking, people tend to avoid reality. An example would be the recommendation in many self-help books not to watch, read, or listen to the news because it is so bad and influences us in negative ways. So should we bury our heads in the sand and live in a fantasy world that everything is beautiful and nice? Should we turn our backs on the starving children of the world? Should we disown our friends if they are going through tough times and speak of their negative issues because they lower our mood? Should we ignore our forests that are being destroyed by pollution or the cutting down of trees? Do you really only want to know the good news? If you only deal with the good and positive in life, ask yourself why.

Positive thinking and believing you can change your life is a realistic ambition if you are willing to commit yourself to the goals. But your success will require more than positive thinking. This requires hard work, long hours, a willingness to fail and try again, and learning to follow your instincts as well as being intellectually tuned in to many possibilities and ways of thinking.

Self-Help Workshop or Cult Meeting?
Crossing the Line

By the time I attended my next self-help workshop, I was getting clarity on marketing schemes used to lure participants into signing up for these events. I began to see the power I was giving away by participating in them. By Saturday night of this weekend, I had enough of being told what to do and how to do it. I also did not want to touch other people's bodies as instructed to do. If I wanted this type of group interaction, I would have signed up for another type of event. This was not about being uncomfortable. I am not shy and I'm very comfortable about my sexuality. This was about setting a boundary and not allowing it to be eroded by peer pressure or anyone else: I decided to leave.

After walking out of the room, a supervisor approached me in the hallway. She tried to talk me out of leaving by accusing me of being afraid to see my "real truth". She made statements about my insecurity and my failure to understand the true meaning of the event. I explained that I was very clear on my real truth and therefore I was leaving because I did not agree with the "truth" shared by the leaders in this weekend of self-growth. As a matter of fact, I knew from my own research that some of the information presented at the workshop was not factual at all. I was upset that a female leader in this position of guiding others knew so little about the subject. I was appalled by the lack of concrete information and clear direction during the whole event.

I felt very sorry for myself and the participants who had paid $1000 or more to attend the workshop. Interestingly, the event started on Friday night with the male counterpart of the female leader stating that the group had been accused of being a cult, but that is was not true. After spending over 24 hours in the group, I would say that it is a cult, but has concealed its agenda of control in subtle ways. The male leader had an ego larger than the hotel we were staying at and his followers worshipped the ground he walked on. He was also a known hypocrite as he gave advice on having a successful monogamous, long-term relationship, yet was cheating on his present partner. Participants went along with whatever they were told and any disagreeing statements were quickly dismissed. Those who didn't comply were shown the door and sent home.

Crossing the Line/Boundaries With Mind Altering Plants/Drugs (when it contains DMT)

Some spiritual gurus recommend the use of plant brews for expanding your consciousness and helping you to transform and heal. The current brew being recommended by spiritual gurus is ayahuasca. This plant mixture is used to alter one's state of consciousness. It is referred to as a spiritual healer, a teacher. Hallucinogens (peyote, magic mushrooms, LSD) toy with the brain in ways that some call spiritual. They may give you a lot of mind-blowing hallucinations that definitely would change the way you see things. But clarity comes with being sane, living in the moment, not in your dreams. An altered state of consciousness can be achieved in spiritual but drug-free ways; for example, ceremonial dancing for 24 hours, hypnosis, or meditation. If you are intent on altering your state of consciousness, why not do it without plant preparations and all the ill effects? If you chose a mind-altering substance, then I question your real motivation. If you just want an excuse for getting stoned, just be honest about it. Cut the excuses, justifications, and rationalizations.

Participants are told that ayahuasca is safe because it has been used by the native people of South America for thousands of years and we can see that these people are just fine. They may not be fine at all. Where are the brain scans to prove this? My belief about this plant brew or any drug use does not require research and studies. It is common sense. When you put something into your body that alters your perceptions, causes hallucinations, vomiting, or diarrhea, and affects your brain in some form or fashion, it is not good for your brain and body health. What happened to the common sense practice of "listening to your body" and paying attention when the body says, No?

We do not have any evidence to show the short or long term effects of ayahuasca. Are you willing to play Russian roulette with your brain and body health? Do not ask for "evidence" from the ones promoting it since there are profits in it for them in one way or another and use it themselves, so they have a biased opinion. It is vital not to give your power away when the consequences involve your mental and physical well-being. You decide what you will do and what you will put into your body and why. Do not buy the sales pitch of others. Remember: Just because the crowd or an individual guru does something or believes something, does not make it right for you. Just because certain people have been doing it for thousands of years does not make it harmless. You must draw the line and claim your strength to decide your own destiny. Think for yourself. Set your boundaries wisely.

Do we have to go along with the crowd to be loved and accepted?

To be authentic, wouldn't it be best to find your inner strength without drugs?

The Miracle Cure & the Placebo Effect

If you are told something has healing powers and you accept this or are open to experimenting, then chances are it will heal you. After all, you "direct your consciousness" when using ayahuasca, just like you can control your dreams and be the director of those. If you believe that you will become more self-aware and that you'll transform your life, then you probably will. Scientists call this the placebo effect. If you want to believe that having cancer makes you more aware and a better person, it will. If you believe jumping off a bridge will help you find clarity in your life, then maybe it will - if you live through it. Beliefs are powerful and can work miracles in people's lives. But that doesn't mean that you should trust something to work just because you're told that it will cure you or help you to change your life. Nor should you take substances or do things that can cause you harm. It you don't know if there is a risk, are you willing to experiment with your own brain, or health, or life, to find out? Remember also, there is no guarantee that your reaction will be the same as someone else's.

The Self-Improvement Workshop
When do they go too far?

I have attended workshops that opened my eyes, made me think differently, and educated me with the best knowledge that we have at the moment. I have come away with a feeling of "money well spent". However, it's important that the "buyer beware" in this realm just like any other realm.

Consider your boundaries and when you're giving away your power when confronted with the hooks for buying a program. Beware of weekend self-improvement workshops that make big promises of transforming your life. There are tricks of the trade to get you hooked and lower your resistance to being manipulated socially and emotionally so that you can be influenced by the "new" training system or program. Remember, someone is making money from your vulnerabilities. Draw a line!

1. The hook. The marketing trick commonly used to attract us to these workshops is to get us hooked by peaking our curiosity. We want to find out the secret method that will be given to us to change our lives. But first you have to sign up, commit to the rules of the program, and pay big money to find out the secrets that no one else knows.

2. Scarcity: Playing to the fear of missing out. Sales tactics to get you to sign up now and pay the money are used at a free introductory session as well as the next workshop you attend. Pressure tactics are common such as using scarcity, "Only four places left", "Sign up at the back of the room at the break as quickly as you can … only ten spots left", "Buy tonight and get this special offer of $$$ instead of the regular price of $$$$$$$." "That's a savings of $$$$."

3. Testimonials. Marketers use testimonials of people who took the course and will tell you how the experience changed or improved their lives. We all do this. But the hook is that you are never told what is in the course. This goes back to the first point regarding curiosity as a hook.

Word of mouth and testimony of an incredible experience is wonderful as long as the participants are not told what and how to express the information they share.

4. Watch out for the lofty claims and rationalization of the expensive workshop such as: "Aren't you worth it? Want to transform your life? Find your true love? Make all your dreams come true!"

5. Rules set the stage. Usually you are asked to commit to the rules and give up your power. This is another red flag. If you chose not to follow the rules, are you asked to leave? Well of course you are because your influence may encourage others who felt the same as you but did not have the courage to say so. Standing up to the authority figures would open the door for others to follow your lead. This could jeopardize the whole workshop event. By word of mouth after the weekend, the company could be put out of business.

6. Lack of sleep makes our brains susceptible to outside influence. We have less energy to resist peer pressure and influence. Thinking becomes a huge challenge when sleep deprived. So look at the agenda and see if you are allowed to sleep the normal eight hours a night. Are you working on workshop exercises and training more than eight hours a day? Do you have downtime? Do you have alone time to reflect and consider the day's events?

7. Restricted menu. I experienced dietary restrictions at a weekend workshop where only vegan food was served. I had no problem with this, but I saw others who felt very differently. Generally, no caffeine or no sugar was served. This translates into less mental energy to resist the manipulation games. You are told that the nutritious food and lack of junk food is good for your health. All true. What is not explained is why the stimulants like sugar and caffeine are not available. These would boost your mental

energy and may provoke you to actually think for yourself and be less susceptible to being a follower. This would not be good for the guru's business. You must be convinced that what you are being taught is the best thing on earth. Usually alcohol and smoking are also restricted. Alcohol would make it more difficult for the leaders to control your behaviour.

Self-Help Workshop Assessment Exercise
Learning from Past Experience to Avoid Making Future Mistakes

- Did the workshop facilitators use peer pressure to manipulate your behaviour?
- Did you normally say, "Yes" to the requests?
- If you didn't choose to follow the rules or the crowd, were you made to feel inadequate some way? (Maybe you were told, "You are feeling threatened and insecure" or "You are not self-aware.")
- Would you consider yourself to be a follower or a leader? It takes a strong secure person to stand up and go against peer pressure.
- Do you have the inner strength to stand alone and say, "No" when the crowd is saying, "Yes?" Do you have the inner strength to not be persuaded by others?
- Did the person running this workshop "walk the talk"? Did this instructor or trainer have the real life experience that gives them the authority to speak from? Did this person have the education to support their claims, messages, and perspectives?
- Was your health ever put at risk? Did you get proper food, sleep, and exercise or at least some form of movement such as an opportunity to go out for a walk? Were you asked to take a drug? Did you go along with the group? If you said "No" were there any consequences?

- Was the cost reasonable?
- Were the claims of benefits reasonable? For example, were you told that this information would transform you into a millionaire? Maybe it would, but the information on becoming a millionaire is not top-secret information that you need to pay an exorbitant amount for.
- Were there secrets about the workshop that would not be revealed until you attended?
- How strict were the rules? Could you abide by them without compromising your boundaries?

Buyer Beware
Choose Your Expert Carefully

Do you want to put yourself in a position of turning your power over to someone else's agenda and beliefs? Is this really gaining your personal power? Who is making the money? Who's ego are you feeding when you comply and do as you are told? Do you want to be a follower? Are you ready to buy into something that you're told is the absolute "truth"?

Do not get fooled into being a follower of something that is not right for you. Do your homework. Know yourself! Study Chapter Two to get more clarity about who you are. Whatever you do, be alert for the jargon mentioned earlier: "Never, always, must, have to, and know." The word "know" sounds so definitive. I have read and heard many experts in the pseudoscience field use scientific terms along with the vocabulary of "proven" or "we now know". No, we do not know all the answers. Someone may be lying to us. Just because an "expert" uses big scientific words does not mean this person is smarter than you or has any absolute answers. It could be that this person is just a con artist good at marketing a product. If you chose to believe an "expert" and buy the program and products, ask yourself who is really benefitting.

The bottom line is: Spend your money wisely on products

and services that resonate with you and support your beliefs and values, and experiment before buying into anything, hook, line and sinker. Stand strong in the face of popular fads. There are many fads that are full of untruths, lack common sense, and have the force of peer pressure behind them. The majority of people find it easier to go along with the status quo or what is "popular" in mainstream society. This is where you need to be as clear as possible about who you are. Draw the lines and set your boundaries. There are wonderful programs and products worth spending your money on. Be wise and know what you think is worth the investment.

Conclusion

It's a good idea to be aware of all kinds of theories and opinions to help you in life. But do not assume that everything you come across is the absolute truth. Look at the information from different points of view. I believe passionately in the messages I have to share. But I don't pretend to be an expert in any field. You may not agree with the stances I take on the issues raised in this chapter or in the rest of this book. My point in sharing my views is for you to consider what feels right for you and make sure your boundaries are set for that. I can't advise you about what's right for you in your life. I can only be the expert on what works for me in my own life.

Finding your "expertise" on your life may take some work. Be open to suggestions. Think through new ideas. Experiment before deciding. Allow yourself to change your mind as you grow and mature with experience. The most important message here is to think for yourself and decide what is best for you. No one else can know what is exactly right for you. The best expert for your life is looking at you in the mirror. Listen to what that person staring back at you has to say. If you need help sorting yourself out, by all means, seek out support, whether by talking to professionals, reading a stack of self-help books, or searching out a variety of true experts. Just remember in the end to listen to yourself and only "own" what works for you.

Do not give away your power to others.

Be the expert of your own life.

Chapter 2
Getting Clear on Who You Are

If you want to see someone in real pain, watch someone who knows who he is and defaults on it on a regular basis.

Pat Murray

The first step for setting healthy boundaries in your life is to know who you are! I want to state this point loud and clear because many of us say or do things in our lives that don't reflect who we really are. Maybe you can recall a time when you completely disagreed with someone in your family, or in your workplace or community, but you went along with it anyway. Why did you make that decision? How does it make you feel when you go against your own wisdom? There are plenty of reasons why you might want to say "Yes" when you would rather say "No". Maybe it's to protect a job that's on the line or save a relationship from collapsing, even though your agreement does not support or even conflicts with your values and beliefs. Sometimes we do this unconsciously, but we know at a gut level when we're going against the guidance that comes from our inner self. The problem with going with the flow when it feels wrong is that you're probably doing things according to boundaries that were set by someone else. This means that you're living your life by default, not by intention or conscious choice. It's only when you make choices that honour your core beliefs that you'll be able to grow and lead a truly fulfilling life.

In this chapter, we'll take a look at how our belief system influences our perspective and behaviour when it comes to relating to others. Getting more clarity about your beliefs in relation to your inner self is the foundation for setting boundaries that really work. I'll share some stories from my own life journey as well as the stories of clients I've worked with in my health consulting practice. As a health and wellness counsellor, I understand the importance of not only knowing who you are but also expressing that real self in constructive and respectful ways. I have seen the price that people pay when living by default, according to someone else's wishes, rather than taking charge and making choices that respect their own integrity. To get your needs met in life and have the life you really want, it's vital to get enough self-awareness to set healthy boundaries for yourself.

Getting to Know YOU

Know thyself. Before we can be clear with anyone else, whether it's a partner, one of our children, a business colleague, or people we just happen to meet along the way, we need to be clear within ourselves about who we are. That means getting in touch with our core beliefs and knowing where we want to draw the line to be true to those beliefs. Even acknowledging our confusion when confronted with an issue that challenges our beliefs is a way of being honest with those around us. Maybe it's time to take a closer look at who you are right now.

Who are you?

Here are some questions to jumpstart the process. At this point in time, what do you know for sure? Do you know who you are? What are your intentions? Do you stand tall and strong in your beliefs? Do you live a life of integrity? What do you care about? Who do you love?

You can see how it's not always easy to answer questions about who you are with complete certainty. Part of the difficulty in getting clarity on ourselves is that we change our views as we go through life. There are stages when our clarity fails due to new experiences and the forces of maturity.

Where do your ideas and beliefs come from?

Let's start by looking at who you are on the surface – at the level of your beliefs and values. The British scientist Richard Dawkins coined the word "memes" to describe the way that ideas and beliefs "replicate themselves from brain to brain," or from person to person. They're like a virus, very contagious. The ideas transmitted to us by our social environment (from our parents, teachers, media etc.,) become apparent in our behaviour and the choices we make in life. They are not actually "choices" if we have been programmed to think a certain way. Ideas and beliefs are passed down from one generation to the next, often without being challenged. Those people that do challenge the beliefs of a culture are deemed social outcasts. Weeding out resistance helps to ensure that the beliefs of the majority continue to live on regardless of whether true or false, right for the times or out of date.

I challenge you to question your beliefs and values to see how they influence your behaviour and the choices you make in your life. Where did your beliefs come from? Which of your beliefs do you want to hold onto? Which ones could use some tweaking? Which ones do you want to discard? Here are some examples to get you started.

1. **The Worker Meme**. What memes or ethical beliefs influence your behaviour in relation to work? The work ethic is deeply ingrained in our society. The meme or cultural belief is that a good person is someone who works hard and makes personal sacrifices to achieve society's highest standard. Our culture places tremendous value on financial success and material rewards. Many people are driven to achieve great wealth to win the approval of others, often at the expense of their health and their personal relationships. Look at people you know who are workaholics. Maybe you're a workaholic yourself. What

drives people to work so hard? Sometimes you'll see a generational pattern – a workaholic meme – when you look at a workaholic's parents and grandparents. What are the beliefs that support that behaviour? Are you a better person if you work seven days a week, 14 hours a day? Does it make you more successful? What is your definition of success? When you answer those questions, think about where your answer is coming from. Where did you get your beliefs about work? Did you learn them from your father? Your education? Your boss? The media? Does your worker meme support who you truly are? Does it give you what you want in your life?

2. **Religion as a Choice?** Religion thrives on memes. We teach our children at a young age while their brains are receptive to absorbing our cultural beliefs without questioning them. This is how religion perpetuates itself from generation to generation. The same applies to any belief system passed from one generation to another. So what do you believe in? Think about what kind of spiritual values your parents taught you, or what you learned about religion in church when growing up. Our ethical system in North America is based on Christian values. It used to be that everyone went to church on Sunday morning to be a "good" person. Things have changed a lot since then. How do we measure a good person these days? Maybe the ideas you learned as a child still hold true for you today. Or maybe you've changed your beliefs or you're in the midst of questioning them. Have you done research into the various schools of thought to decide which spiritual path to follow, if any? Are you aware of the scientific research on mystical experiences? In recent decades, scientists have explored the connection between spirituality and brain function. They discovered that spiritual feelings activate a part of the brain that triggers chemicals to create a calming

effect. Meditation has this effect on the mind-body. Maybe that's a new area you'd like to explore.

3. **The Spotless House Syndrome**. Many of you may have been raised, like myself, to keep a clean house. Although traditional gender roles have relaxed a lot, today's women still carry the burden of housecleaning. Why do I feel the need to keep my house so clean? Besides the obvious need for some cleanliness in maintaining our homes, our society has attached the idea that a "good" wife, mother, woman works hard at keeping her house clean. The cleaner it is the more gold stars beside her name. She gets the stamp of approval by society because she has succeeded in meeting its social standards. So do I feel better living in a clean house because it is actually clean? Or do I feel better because it makes me socially acceptable? Maybe I have reasons of my own for keeping my personal space clean, such as my brain works better in a well-organized, dirt-free environment. Some brain types love to work in a messy place. How do we know whether we're living according to our own values or someone else's? Who is that "someone else"? Have I challenged this meme within myself? The point I want you to consider here is whether or not your behaviour honours and supports your own values.

4. **The Marriage Meme**. For many people, marriage is a big ethical issue. It can be a problematic meme because of people's conflicting beliefs. The definition of what a marriage "should" be like can vary dramatically from culture to culture. Take polygamy; for example, the practice of taking many wives. What's okay for one religious group may be completely taboo for another. Not long ago, people didn't challenge the institution of marriage the way we do today. It was a given that when you grew up you'd get married and have a family. These days, the high divorce rate reflects a shift in our values. Same-sex marriage is

becoming acceptable. Yet, who knows? Society may revert back to the old ways in a generation or two. Regardless of social background, couples don't always see eye to eye when it comes to expressing their core values and beliefs in marital life. Which memes do you live by in your marriage or choose to live by if you get married or partner with someone? The marriage roles and customs taught to you by your parents? By your religion? By your community? Are you really happy living your love life the way others say you should? If you could throw out the memes you've been given and start all over, what would your love life and your intimate relationships look like?

Memes & Me
How do you know which memes to choose?

Sometimes it's tough deciding which beliefs you want to accept as your own and which ones you need to throw out because they don't actually work for you. If you're living your life according to spoon-fed beliefs, values, and behaviours, chances are you're not being all you could be in life. Maybe it's time to examine what you've been taught to be true and do some research. That's one of the best ways to find out who you are. You could start by taking a closer look at some of the areas we've discussed: your standard of cleanliness, your work ethic, your views on marriage and religion. How do your beliefs line up with the mainstream belief system? After some reflection, decide which memes you really want to hang onto and which ones you'd like to let go. Acting on the new beliefs that replace your old ones can be very scary, especially if you're going against the social norms. This process is well worth the effort because by doing it, you get to be the real you and live your very unique life.

Here's a clue to finding out whether you really support the values you're living by. Look to see if there's a disconnection between what you say you believe and your actions in life. An example would be someone who claims to be a Christian yet commits adultery and rationalizes this behaviour. If this person is going against the rules and values of Christianity, then chances are, he or she is not a true believer. Living up to one's actual beliefs means that they're reflected in one's behaviour, and it's not a façade. That would be living a life of true integrity. Being true to your real self translates into authenticity.

Facing the Tiger
What fears need to be addressed before you can move forward?

We all have fears about different issues throughout our lives. How we deal with those fears may depend on how we feel about ourselves. What's keeping you from doing and being all that you want to in life? Are you able to name your fears? Fear of failure? Fear of being alone? Fear of getting hurt? Walk up to the tiger that's getting in your way, the fear that's keeping you from taking on a new challenge or moving your life in a new direction. Chances are it will turn out be out to be a kitten, just a negative belief you're holding about yourself that isn't true at all.

Facing your fears is a good way to see who's pulling the strings. Let's say that you'd like to go back to college and finish your degree or start a new course of study, but you're afraid you'll never be a success at it. Where do you get that idea? Your partner? Your father? It's even harder to take on a new challenge that could help you to change your life in a positive way when someone close to you doesn't believe in you enough to support your decision. But most of our self-doubts can be traced to negative feedback that we pick up all the time in living our lives, "You're not good enough, you're not pretty enough, you're not rich enough" and so on. Says who? Who says you can't do it? It's likely that those doubts in your mind come from listening to what others say, not from your inner guidance.

The people pleaser: Some of my clients discover that it's fear of displeasing others that causes them to do things that aren't healthy for them. One of the biggest reasons that a person becomes a people pleaser comes from the fear of not being loved by the people in their life. A symptom would be to immediately answer incoming text messages and emails at three o'clock in the morning rather than waiting a few hours until eight o'clock. If you're a people pleaser, you may have low self-esteem. Maybe you find yourself thinking that you're not as good or as lucky as others. Where did this self-doubt come from? There's probably a meme lurking in there somewhere. Are you able to see when you act out of low self-esteem? A symptom of low self-esteem would be the constant need for finding sexual validation from one partner after another. Maybe you're someone who finds yourself saying "Yes" to most everyone when you're asked to do something. Did you ever ask yourself why you don't say "No" instead? When you say, "Yes" and it's not what you really want, then that's not a true reflection of who you are. No one can feel empowered by constantly being a "Yes person". Take charge and change.

Hold your ground. Think of a time when you stood your ground and didn't allow others to take advantage of you. Wasn't that empowering? Do it more often.

Trust your inner guidance. A people pleaser can gain self-esteem by learning to trust in their own judgment rather than depending on others when making decisions.

Love who you are. To get beyond the fear of not being loved and accepted, learn to accept and love who you are right now.

Follow your heart. Instead of listening to someone else or following the crowd, try following the guidance of your heart instead.

Peer Pressure - at All Ages
How can you escape conformity and be yourself?

We are social creatures who are influenced by those around us. Chose very carefully who your friends are and how you spend your time. You will morph with those around you regardless of how strongly you feel that you will not, no matter how strong your identity. This tendency has been confirmed by research in behavioral psychology. As Daniel Amen, M.D., advises us: "Nurture your relationships because you become like the people you spend time with."

When you evaluate who you are and who you want to be, it's possible that you'll have to set some abrupt and strong boundaries for interacting with those around you. This may mean that you completely end and disconnect from certain relationships or groups that diminish you. It may also mean that you nurture relationships that are good for you and enhance who you are. Reaching out to find new friends and joining groups with common goals and values will help to support you as you find your way. People are happiest when living a life of purpose with other like-minded individuals.

We tend to link the phrase "peer pressure" with teenagers. Generally, when we hear about peer pressure it pertains to the negative influences challenging teenagers' lives. The media feature endless stories about drugs, alcohol, car accidents, bullying, and sex – all related to teens. I would like to point out that those highly influential years also can produce some very positive results in teen behaviour. I want to share a couple of stories about a teenager named Kevin, whom I happen to know very well. This young man has been a positive influence on his peers.

Kevin is a highly motivated teenager involved in two different sports, marksmanship and biathlon; he competes at both provincial and national levels. He made the Canadian team and will compete at an international competition in England in 2013. Last year after being away for a week competing in biathlon, I asked Kevin if there was a lot of alcohol and drugs at the party events during the week. He said, "You don't get it. Athletes who are serious about winning don't risk their performance the next day by getting intoxicated the night before. Those that do are not making it to the next level. Eventually it catches up with them." Kevin has always stood up to his peers on this subject. It would be my guess that most will ignore Kevin's message, though, I know of at least one situation where Kevin's influence did make a difference. How many others that have heard him go on and on about why not to do drugs and alcohol have re-considered their choices? All it takes is one person to get up and take a stand. Many will follow a strong leader. Followers need leaders who are not afraid to go against the popular flow. Kevin is a leader. He does what he believes is right, upfront, loud, and clear. He is confident – sometimes to a fault and surpasses many adults on this point. Kevin is driven to do right and stands alone if need be. His peers are drawn to him for this reason. I am thankful that this young man is influencing others to be better people. This same kind of personality could be used in negative and destructive ways.

When Kevin was in the eighth grade, he decided he was going to dress a certain way that was not popular at school. He chose to wear dressier clothes to get the "dress for success" look. After a few weeks, he had started a new trend. Others were following his lead. Of course, the girls flocked to him, not because of his style of clothes, but because of his confidence and his ability to stand out in a crowd as the leader, the strong one.

What I love best about Kevin is his strong ability to set clear boundaries and not allow others to erode them away. This is definitely unusual for a fifteen-year-old. As his mother, it will be interesting to see how he evolves over time and what kind of leader he will turn out to be in the future.

Kevin sets a great example for being strong in who you are and not allowing others to trample on your values. If only everyone, at every age, could be this clear and this willing to set boundaries to stand up for who they are and what they believe.

Finding Yourself Means Creating Yourself

I love the concept of creating yourself because it makes us accountable and responsible for our lives. Rather than wandering around aimlessly in the dark, waiting to find ourselves, or blaming others for who we are, and going through the same old act day in, day out, we can reach out of our box, experiment, and make choices that create the person we want to be. The best thing I ever did when I needed to find myself and create a new life for myself was to go out and try new things.

Step outside your comfort zone

Try new things, many new things. Some will stick, and some will be a flop. Don't worry about the outcome. How will you know who you are and what you want until you entertain new ideas and decide what new thoughts to act on?

Get high on a recreational activity

To begin creating a new life for myself, I tried out many sports activities ranging from kayaking, dragon boat racing, sailing, and cross country skiing, to cycling, running, and gym workouts. Hiking, cycling, cross-country skiing, and kayaking really resonated with me and have become part of my life. These aerobic activities release chemicals in my body that trigger feelings of peace and well-being. I feel the euphoric "high" that people talk about. Some people say that they have this spiritual kind of experience with music or art. The important message here is that you find things to do in life that touch your soul and make you feel spiritually connected to yourself as well as to the world.

Change your clothes and change your self-image

I have been fairly conservative in my dress and places I go for entertainment. One day, I bought an outfit that was a little more revealing, tighter than my normal dress, and went out for karaoke and dancing. For some women this may be no big deal, but for me it was out of my box, way out of my comfort zone. I tried something new. Did it work for me? Absolutely! I had so much fun. Ever since, I have been updating my wardrobe with a wider variety of clothes to express how I feel about myself. Does this mean I no longer wear my sharp black business suit? No! It means I dress for the occasion. Simply experimenting with something so simple as my usual type of dress caused me to re-think who I was and what message I wanted to communicate to others.

What would happen if the conservative businessman traded in his subdued tie for one that was colorful and outrageous compared to the usual drab business tie? What would happen if the salesman went home after work and instead of putting on his baggy sweats to lie on the sofa and watch TV, he put on sailing clothes and went out to take some lessons. He might love the experience so much that he'd decide to crew on a race boat. Maybe this would work for him, maybe not, but at least he would be doing something different to find out what he really liked, wanted, or needed.

Join a club and surprise yourself.

When you reach out to participate in a new realm, you really never know what will come of it. The experience may be positive or negative, but either way, you will learn and grow from it. I also tried the adventure of joining the public speaking club Toastmasters. This activity also stuck with me. What I learned about myself through the leadership challenges at Toastmasters was an unexpected surprise. After serving in several executive roles, I could clearly see where my strengths and weaknesses were. This gave me clarity on what I needed to work on for management skills. I greatly improved my public speaking skills, and in ways I had not anticipated. I had felt my strong suit was in prepared speeches. I soon learned I had a propensity for impromptu speaking and became the Provincial Champion in

2011. I grew more from my experiences speaking in these clubs than I ever imagined possible. The old saying, "You get out of it what you put into it" applies. All of these lessons came to me because I stepped out of my box to try something new.

Caution: Put on your parachute.

Bear in mind that when it comes to trying out new things and stepping out of your comfort zone, it's important to listen to your instincts to decide what's right for you. Sometimes your fear is giving you advice that you should pay close attention to before taking the plunge. "Feel the fear and do it anyway"? No! Stop! Fear is there for a reason. It's one thing to force yourself to step onto the stage to overcome a common fear like public speaking. It's quite another to take on a big challenge before you're ready.

We human beings are programmed to intuit fear for the purpose of survival. If we are feeling afraid or anxious and our intuition is screaming at us that something doesn't "smell right," it's because there may be a tiger waiting in the bushes to eat us. Rather than charging ahead with blind determination saying, "I am going to do it anyway," stop and analyze what the fear is about. Draw a line by admitting to yourself that you feel the fear, understand where it's coming from, and choose not to change the situation until you're ready. It's better to be in a safe space and make a plan that's doable before embracing the change you want. Balance the fears with due diligence. Jumping out of a plane without a parachute is not recommended.

For example, a person who faces their fear about going into business for themselves and does so without proper preparation and research could end up in a financial disaster.

Changing How Others Treat Us by Setting Our Boundaries

The way we allow others to treat us is something we can

change. We cannot control other people's behaviour, but we can set boundaries for ourselves about what we will or will not tolerate. We can change their behaviour toward us by changing our own way of relating and model a healthier way to relate and communicate.

The following story illustrates how one of my clients was able to improve his life by setting healthy boundaries in his style of communication. Nick came to me for advice on nutrition and reducing his stress level, and discovered that the source of his stress was directly related to how he interacted with his partner.

Nick and Mary

When Mary criticized and belittled Nick, he would go silent and not respond, hoping she would stop and the conflict would end. Instead her verbal abuse continued. Finally Nick had enough and said, "I know you are hurting and striking out at me. Your verbal attacks hurt me also and I need you to find another way of dealing with your pain. Would you be willing to go to counselling for help either on your own or together with me?"

Nick was setting a boundary to show that he would not tolerate being attacked by Mary anymore. At the same time, he was reaching out to help her, and them, solve the problem. He drew a line with respect and love, rather than striking back to hurt her in return, which is a very immature way of dealing with conflict.

When dealing with criticism, it is best not to change the subject to avoid discussion and verbally hit the other person back. This only ignites a war: "You hit me so I will hit you back". That's two-year-old mentality. Let's put on our "big boy pants and our big girl panties" and behave like mature adults. Stay with the points made and find out if they are true or just verbal attacks made out of anger, hurt, or frustration. Look at yourself and ask if the criticism is justified. This may be difficult to do in the heat of the moment and when you feel hurt. Be honest with yourself and the other person. Admit your faults. Take responsibility for anything you may have done to create the problem. Then decide if these are things you are willing to change or not.

This may take some time to think about. Tell your partner you need to think over the points that they made and you will get back to them after you have had time to consider whether or not they are true. This also gives both of you some cooling off time.

Decide whether or not you are willing to put in the effort to change some of the issues that are bothering your partner. This is where you make a decision to set boundaries for yourself and communicate these in a calm and respectful way.

Be flexible to a point that is appropriate for the situation but not so flexible you lose yourself and end up with having your boundaries erased. How far does your line of flexibility stretch? When have you given too much and lost yourself? When have you stretched too much and snapped?

Setting Respectful Boundaries
Not Bullying the Other Person

There are people who may run with the concept of setting boundaries in a negative way. Think very carefully when you draw a line if you are doing so for the right reasons. Please do not misinterpret the concept of "setting boundaries" and put a negative spin on boundary setting by using it for negative purposes.

If you're using this strategy to control or manipulate others, seek advice from a professional counsellor to help you create healthy boundaries for your relationships. That way of handling your control issues is not the lesson on boundaries I'm trying to get across in this book. If you are using the jargon to justify being stubborn or closed-minded, again, seek help. It is extremely difficult, if not impossible, to recognize these traits in yourself. This is where talking to an experienced and properly trained professional can help. (Chose your "professional people" carefully and wisely. Look into background credentials before paying your hard-earned money to someone who is not qualified and not "walking the talk.") If you are mature and self-aware enough to see and acknowledge your minuses as well as your pluses, then you may be capable of analyzing whether or not your boundary setting is balanced and realistic.

Be respectful when stating who you are and what you want. Drawing a line and standing strong is a positive step forward. Learning to hold your ground with love and kindness may take some practice.

Be aware that when you change your behaviour and request to be honoured for your new way of relating and communicating, others may feel threatened or fearful. Or others may not accept this new you and it may lead to the end of your relationship with them. Situations that may be particularly difficult are with children, teenagers, and partners. It will take a lot of inner strength to stand up for yourself to request that your boundaries be respected, and not waver when pulled in different directions by those we love and want in our lives. Change can be very painful. It can also be very empowering and liberating because we are being true to ourselves.

Using the Power of Intention v. Living by Default

When you know who you are, what you want, and why, living with intention flows. When your clarity is muddy, that's when going along with the crowd or the people around you is easy. There is no reason to not go with the flow of others because you have no intentions for your own life. How could boundaries possibly be set if your intentions are not clear to even you? Hence, living a life of default. Your power is not lost, but never has come to the surface.

The other possibility is that you may have been living a life full of intention and then been disempowered due to various reasons and situations. Maybe you were challenged on your boundaries and had them eroded while thinking you were doing the best thing.

During the first 16 years of my marriage, I set the intention of being successful in that relationship. After many years of struggling and coming to a place of hopelessness, that intention eroded away to a life of default. This meant not living life to its fullest with passion, motivation, and happiness. I spent years living in what I call the grey zone. It was depressing and sucked the life right out of me. My joy was gone. Life was a daily grind. My children were tired of being around a depressed, stressed, and exhausted mom. The unhappiness in me could not be camouflaged.

The diagnosis of breast cancer was the huge kick in the "heart" to jumpstart my determination to live, once again, with intention. I had to much fear as I knew that this health crisis would probably bring me to the decision of leaving my husband. Before I did this, I exhausted all possibilities. Nothing worked after nine years. When the pain of staying in the relationship became greater than the pain of leaving, and it was extremely painful, then it was clear that drastic measures had to be taken. It is very sad to think that I had to leave this relationship in order to be heard. I had to remind myself many times a day, by consulting a list, who I was, what I needed, and how I would not settle any longer. Living with intention was my theme then and still is today.

With clarity about your intention comes the next step, setting the boundaries. I am clear about my boundaries and will not allow them to be trampled to pieces again.

Margaret Thatcher (according to the movie version of her life) explained to her future husband that she loved him terribly, but would never be the domestic housewife. She drew a very strong line because she understood herself and was not going to settle for a life of not being true to herself. Thatcher followed her beliefs and passions, living a life of intention, regardless of whether or not others agreed with or supported her. She did not allow herself to be compromised – a lesson that I learned the hard and painful way. *Do not allow yourself to be compromised!*

Do not allow yourself to be compromised by the needs and demands of others at the expense of your own.

Do not allow yourself to be compromised by playing a role that's not true to yourself.

Do not allow yourself to be compromised by giving your precious time and energy to support those who can't or won't reciprocate.

With self-awareness, comes an understanding of your own strengths as well as your limitations, along with a greater ability to accept the strengths and limitations of others. The key to a strong healthy relationship with another person is to find the balance between the needs and desires of both of you.

Learning to Compromise with Flexibility

All too often, the concept of compromise is misunderstood. Compromising with another person does not mean giving in. It means giving something in order to come to a mutual agreement, but not giving up everything you hold important. It does not mean giving up who you are. Compromise reflects the ability to be flexible in order to make relationships work.

The challenge is in deciding to what extent you are willing to be flexible. If you "flex" too much in order to please others or out of fear of rejection, then you have lost yourself. You may be left with feelings of defeat and loss rather than satisfaction and strength. Compromise should feel like a "win, win" not a "win, lose."

When you allow for flexibility, you still can stand strong with integrity. Your power will not be diminished if you don't allow your core boundary lines to be eroded. When considering how flexible you want to be in making a compromise with someone, listen to your gut. How do you feel? Comfortable, respected, valued, and enhanced? Or disillusioned, hurt, degraded, and diminished? What are your conditions for compromise? What are the conditions of the agreement, the "if, but, maybe, also, and, or"?

What do you absolutely know for sure?

There are some personal beliefs that I could put on a list knowing that these beliefs may never change. I love my kids. I love the outdoors. This list could be extended to my values regarding nutrition, exercise, money, relationships, or spirituality. However, there are some questions that you could ask me about myself today, yet if you ask me a year from now my answers may have changed. When it comes to our beliefs, the important thing is to leave the door open to changing your mind about what you think is true. New information and new experiences are continually coming into your life. As you grow and mature, it's natural for you to change your ideas if you can remain flexible and open-minded. What do you know for sure and find important to you at this moment in time? Make a list stating your beliefs and values and how you will put them into place.

The Work - Getting Clarity On Who You Are

As you become clear about your self-identity and the boundaries you want to set, keep yourself open to change as you grow and mature. When you answer the questions in the following reflection exercises, remember that your answers will be a reflection of who you are at this point in time. Hopefully, next year, or five or ten years from now, you will have evolved beyond this point. Some of your core values and beliefs may be the same and some may be different. As you go through life, be open to change when it's right for you. That being said, change is difficult and sometimes goes hand in hand with upheaval and crisis. Change goes with the territory when we're on journeys of personal transformation.

Meme work: Identifying Your Values and Beliefs

Make a list of your values and beliefs.

Which ones are "memes"?

Which values and beliefs are you going to keep and claim as your own?

Living with Integrity
Where Are You on a Scale from 1-10?

Although being an honourable person who lives with integrity is not an important goal for everyone, I think that most people would like to say they have these qualities. You may desire to be a person of high integrity, but the question is, does your behaviour reflect it? Confirming its existence in our actions is not always easy. Here, we enter the grey zone.

I like to measure integrity values on a scale of 1-10. No one, in my opinion, can always be a 10. We may have stages in our lives where we would give ourselves a "2," but later we may be at an 8 and then fall back down to a 4. At this point in time, I would give myself a 9/10. In the past, I fell down to 4, and later on in my marriage I fell even further to a 1. When I left the marriage, I felt my integrity go back up to a 9 because I was being very honest and living what I was "preaching".

Rate each value and belief that you list on a scale from 1-10 (1 being the least and 10 being the most) with respect to how you are living up to your own expectations. Do you see some changes you want to make? When and how are you going to do this? What is stopping you?

Create Yourself!

Remember that you have the ability to create the life you want for yourself. Take a good look at yourself and your beliefs to see what you want to change to become the person you want to be and have the life you want to live.

1. Who are you now?
2. What can you do to challenge yourself on who you think you are now?
3. Make a list of things you can do differently. Try brand new things, read different books, explore different topics, learn new information, take classes, eat different foods, exercise with a new sport or a new routine, join a different club, make new friends, try something new in your sex life, be open to surprises, wear something out of your box, try a different type of vacation.
4. Enough thinking … go out and do something – anything, new!
5. Journal what you learn about yourself while experimenting with the novel experiences.
6. What will you choose to keep in your life and what will you discard?

Changing the Way Others Treat Us

How do you "allow" others to treat you? Are you happy with this answer?

What boundaries do you need to set in order to send a clear message about what you will and will not tolerate in regard to how others treat you.

Living with Intention versus by Default

Are you clear about your intentions? What are they? Are you living them?

Are you living a life of default? If so, what are you going to do about it? Anything? When? Why? How? Make the effort to answer these questions in detail.

Code of Ethics

To help get clear about who you are and where you want to set your boundaries, write out your code of ethics. This reflects the intentions for your life. Here is my own code of ethics to use as an example.

As of December 1, 2012

1. I will be a life long learner.
2. I will be financially responsible.
3. I will be the best parent possible for my children.
4. I will strive for professionalism in every aspect of my work.
5. I will strive to communicate constructively and openly with respect and consideration for other people's feelings. When appropriate, I will be a risk taker with forthright conversations that make me vulnerable. I believe this is necessary to establish real and meaningful relationships.
6. I will live a life of intention not default.
7. I will strive to embrace those things that enhance my life, not diminish it.
8. I will strive to live a life of integrity.
9. I will take care of my health in terms of brain, body, and soul.
10. I will not allow others to erode my boundaries.
11. I will stand up for what *I* believe is right for me.
12. I will be there for my loved ones in good times and in bad.
13. I will give and receive equally in all my relationships except with my children. Parents always give more than they receive because they are parents.
14. I will re-evaluate my code of ethics periodically and be open to changing it as I continue to learn, grow, and mature.

Conclusion

The most important lesson of this chapter is to take some time to get to know yourself and then draw boundaries that honour the real you. Flexibility is required to be able to have healthy relationships, but not to the degree that you end up compromising your whole self, your deeper integrity. It's important for you to make it clear where the flexibility is in setting your boundaries. Bear in mind that our personal boundaries are always in a state of flux and evolution because we, ourselves, are always in a state of change and maturity. With greater awareness comes the opportunity to really own your boundaries while honouring those of others.

Chapter 3
Setting Clear Boundaries in Personal Relationships

*Successful relationships require that all parties view
getting their core needs met as being legitimate.*
Susan Scott

The Merriam-Webster Dictionary defines a boundary as "something that indicates or fixes a limit or extent". That definition works fine if we're talking about how fast you can drive your vehicle until going over the speed limit. But when it comes to boundaries in personal relationships, a key concept needs to be added to the definition: evolution. In the process of living our lives, we can evolve beyond the boundaries that define and limit us in our relationships with other people. As our perspective, needs, and values change, we outgrow our old selves. When we see things differently, our boundaries will need to evolve to reflect that. The problem is our boundaries don't always change along with us. We get stuck. Many of us get put in boxes that we ourselves or other people create for us because we want to be loved and accepted. We may feel these boxes will get us exactly that.

In this chapter, we will look at how people can get stuck in limiting and unhappy relationship boxes and what can be done to set them free to be more authentic. These stories are designed to help you decide where to set your boundary lines. How much flexibility can you make room for in your relationships with others before someone crosses a personal boundary line or your line snaps?

Trapped in the Box

In our relationships with other people, we sometimes limit them by placing them in a box. Those imaginary boxes can set really tight boundaries around others. We have certain expectations that a person will behave a certain way. Drawing such rigid boundaries can sabotage growth. It limits a person and ruins the potential for a relationship to evolve. The problem here is that when we paint someone into a space that doesn't fit, we don't allow that person to be who he or she fully is. The lines have been drawn with a thick permanent marker. It's almost like working at an entry-level job where your boss thinks you're only capable of doing what's on the job description. Over time you learn, grow, and mature. Yet the boss is blind to this and you're never allowed to move up the ladder. You have to leave the job to get a promotion. We're fortunate if the people in our lives are not blind to our growth, but sometimes we have to leave a relationship to get that "promotion".

The Marriage Box

Whenever my husband and I had intense conversations about our relationship towards the end of our marriage, I would tell him exactly what I thought and how I felt. He would respond by saying that I was mistaken and he knew what I really thought. He had placed me in a certain box based on an old image he had of me. When I spoke my truth and explained that I had changed, he wouldn't accept the truth. He was convinced that his image of me was the right one. There was no changing his mind. After twenty-three years of married life, I had changed. I had grown and matured and was not the same person he had married. He could not accept or understand me. It was insulting to be told who I was. It was diminishing to speak my truth and not have it believed. I didn't want to get out of the marriage, but I wanted more than anything to get out of the box he had trapped me in for so many years. In the end, I had to leave the relationship to get free to be myself. Looking back on things, I realize that I had done the same thing to my husband. He wanted out of the box, too! Now we both live our separate lives happily "out of the box".

Some couples manage to handle the changes in their lives in a way that allows the relationship to thrive, not fall apart. These couples find acceptance for each other's changes and allow room for self-development. People inevitably change and grow, which means that for a committed relationship to survive, it needs to evolve along with the changes. Each person will have to decide what they can or cannot accept as their partner goes through changes. That will take some reflection along with good communication. Boundaries with partners must be flexible enough for the relationship to grow and evolve. If they are not, the relationship will stagnate and the marriage may have to end.

Taking a Stand in Your Relationships

Regardless of the nature of a relationship, whether it's with your partner, a business colleague, or a close friend, it is your responsibility to know where your boundaries are with regard to your core values and beliefs. How else will you stand up for yourself and what you want in life? It's not the other person's responsibility to figure out where your boundaries are. That person has to be responsible for setting his or her boundaries and you for yours. If someone accuses you of being controlling because you strongly uphold your position on a certain issue and that person does not, that's not your problem. You should be compassionate about the situation, but that doesn't mean you need to give in. Being supportive and honouring someone else's lines is respectful. It does not need to be at the expense of your own. In the spirit of trying to make a relationship work, it's all too easy to give in and lose your boundaries and yourself in the process.

The Importance of Flexibility - How Far to Stretch?

Flexibility is necessary in setting boundaries in our relationships because different relationships and different circumstances may require different boundary lines or different degrees of applying the same boundaries. Be flexible to a point that is appropriate for the situation, but not so flexible that you lose yourself and end up with having your boundaries erased. The challenge is in deciding to what extent you're willing to be flexible. The key here is balance. If you "flex" too much in order to please others or out of fear of rejection, then you have lost yourself. You may be left with feelings of defeat and loss rather than satisfaction and strength.

How far does your line of flexibility stretch? When have you given too much and lost yourself? When have you stretched too much and snapped? Understand your limitations when honouring other people. If the boundaries cause irreconcilable differences and there is no more flexibility left, then a relationship may be over. This is where you need to be really clear on your lines and know your limitations when trying to honour others.

The Meaning of Compromise

All too often, the concept of compromise is misunderstood. Compromise does not mean giving up who you are. Compromise reflects the ability to be flexible in order to make relationships work. Compromise should feel like a "win, win" not a "win, lose". Both parties must give something to enhance the relationship, but not at the expense of their core needs and beliefs.

If a person with strong Christian beliefs was asked to become an atheist, or an atheist was asked to become a Christian, in order for the relationship to exist, this would not be considered a compromise but a request that boundaries be erased. Or if one person wanted a monogamous relationship and the other wanted a non-monogamous relationship, this would be an example of a situation beyond compromise and flexibility. These fundamental kinds of issues are usually deal breakers. If you have agreed to a situation that is in conflict with your core values, your decision will catch up with you sooner or later. Symptoms may be a deep sense of dissatisfaction, unhappiness, resentment, anger, depression, and living a life of default.

Willing versus Have to

Whenever we have a conversation with someone that requires setting our boundaries, it's important to feel that you're *willing* to do something rather than you *have to* because it's expected of you. Ask yourself what you are willing to do. Always ask others what they are willing to do too. No one can be successful in a relationship without applying this concept. It supports freedom and cooperation rather than assuming an attitude that forces someone to do something. As author Susan Scott puts it, "Trying to enforce anything would be like trying to nail Jell-O to the wall" (*Fierce Conversations*).

People Pleasers
Where to Draw the Line?

It often happens in close relationships with others that one person will take on the role of a people pleaser. People pleasers allow others to cross their boundary lines for the sake of maintaining the relationship. That means putting the needs and interests of another person or group ahead of your own needs, values, or desires. This is a common pattern in relationships. It's an example of what happens when you live your life by default and let someone else tell you what to do, rather than making choices that support who you really are and what you really want.

The following examples of people pleasers are drawn from stories shared by my clients. There are many people who go overboard to please others in their close relationships. As different as the people in these stories are, you'll see that the reasons these individuals want so much to please others have a common theme: the desire to be loved and accepted.

People Pleaser #1
Way over the Line!

Mike was a successful breadwinner for his wife and two children. He had to put in at least a 70-hour workweek in order to make the kind of money required to maintain his family's lifestyle. When Mike came home from work at night, the dishes weren't done, the laundry was stacked up, and the place needed cleaning. He described the house as a disaster. Typically, the children had not been properly fed or taken care of. Sometimes he had to go out at eleven o'clock at night to buy groceries and make a meal for his hungry children who should have been in bed. Mike was the one who took the kids to school, drove them to their activities, and coached their sports teams. This was the "normal" state of life for this household. Mike's wife was a stay-at-home mom who believed that her children (who were not yet ten years old) could more or less take care of themselves. Mike, being the dedicated father and husband that he was, ended up emotionally and physically exhausted from serving as breadwinner, caregiver, super dad, and housecleaner. How did Mike get to this place? The short answer: no real boundaries.

Mike had no sense of boundaries when it came to his health and personal needs. Mike was willing to do his utmost to support the needs of his family, but he let himself be totally taken advantage of by his spouse who was not contributing equally to the workload. Mike explained to me in one of our sessions that when he married his wife, he had certain expectations with regard to who was going to take care of what in the relationship. He didn't think about putting their responsibilities into a written agreement or even sitting down with his future wife to have that discussion. As a result, there were no clearly defined roles or boundaries about the responsibilities within the household. That is why Mike got into a place of exhaustion and ended up seeking help from a nutrition counsellor to restore his health.

If the wife is a stay-at-home mom, why isn't she doing most of the domestic chores? At the other extreme, should the traditional male breadwinner come home and not offer any help? I am not suggesting you live your life according to any set of rules based on percentages here. But I would suggest for married couples to come up with a plan that is fair and reasonable to both spouses. What you come up with is a personal matter.

If Mike started setting boundaries, he would soon realize that he was burning himself out both in his health and his career. He would be a much better father, businessperson, and partner if he were not so exhausted. If his partner was unwilling to take on the workload on the domestic front, Mike could set boundaries to limit his own workload by hiring help. A nanny could take care of the children's needs as well as the domestic chores. Though we might wonder, why would he stay married to a woman who did not contribute anything to her family's well being. The last-ditch option for drawing the line in this relationship would be for Mike to say, "No more!" and get a divorce. Mike did in fact end up getting divorced from his wife.

This story is not over. Has Mike learned the lessons of boundary setting from his past marriage? Does he follow through on those boundaries? No. Although Mike is aware of his pattern of not setting boundaries at times, it still pervades his life. His career and his health continue to pay a heavy price.

The Guilt Trip

Rather than sticking to his work, many times Mike provides a taxi service for his now teenage children. These teens are very capable of using public transit and if the situation requires, Mike could order a cab to do the picking up and delivering. Mike's time is worth $250 per hour. A taxi would cost between $30-$50 to meet the needs of any given situation. Money is not the issue.

Mike is overloaded with work that must be done with deadlines. During his workday, he is constantly interrupted by his children's requests, and by friends calling to chat about issues that could be dealt with after work hours. Because Mike is overwhelmed and always behind on his "to do" list, he stays up until three or four o'clock in the morning, pumped up on caffeine or other drugs to keep him awake. Then he crashes for a few hours and gets up feeling like death warmed over and wonders why he can't function well. Being sleep deprived is a regular problem and is wearing on his health and all his relationships. Mike feels guilty for not saying "Yes" to every little request made to him by his children and others. His children say, "Jump Dad!" and Mike says, "How high honey?" Guilt is a black hole. If you suffer from guilt, there are some great self-help books on that subject alone. Start talking to someone about your issue who can help you through the process of giving it up. Setting boundaries must be done guilt free in order for you to stick with the follow through and be consistent in every aspect of your life.

People Pleaser #2
The Jellyfish Syndrome

The following story is another example of a parent who doesn't know how to set healthy boundaries for himself. This lack of boundaries carries over to the way he raises his children without drawing any clear lines. As a role model he doesn't set a good example for his children. How will his children be able to set boundaries for themselves if their father doesn't have good boundaries of his own?

Greg does not take care of himself in regards to sleep, eating, exercise, stress, or his social life. Not a big surprise that his children don't either. There is no consistent bedtime or getting up time in this family. Greg has given the children no guidelines for nutrition, exercise, or how to choose friends. How can Greg explain to his children that going to bed on time and getting a full night's sleep is vital to our moods, emotional health, brain function, and a healthy body, if he's not doing it himself? Greg needs to decide on his own boundaries first and start setting the example.

The next lesson the children learn comes with watching how Greg, their dad, does not stand up to his wife, their mother. Dad does whatever is necessary to keep the mother content. Greg feels like a doormat. The way he allows himself to be treated shows a lack of self-respect. Greg and his wife are now divorced. Greg has deep issues of low self-esteem and guilt that are being addressed with counselling.

One of Greg's teenagers, Trevor, has finished high school. He isn't going to college or university at this time. He has a part-time job, 15 hours a week. Trevor lives with his dad. Trevor plays games on the computer most of his waking day and into the night. Trevor's sleep pattern is all mixed up because of this, so during the day he sleeps a lot unless he has to be at work. Greg is working 70 hours a week. Yet Trevor expects his dad to do all the domestic chores, grocery shopping, and cooking. Dad also pays for all of Trevor's living expenses and play money: it's an easy life for Trevor.

Greg needs to set some ground rules if he is willing to support his child at this age. First of all, his son is perfectly capable of taking a bus instead of being driven around by his dad. Trevor is also capable and has plenty of time to go grocery shopping, cook for both of them, clean the house and help out wherever necessary. Why should his dad be doing all the domestic chores on top of his long work hours? Since Trevor is not participating in helping out, Greg could lighten his load by setting some boundaries and ground rules for living together. And of course, there have to be consequences if Trevor does not respect those rules and boundaries.

I would suggest that Trevor get a full time job, contribute to rent and food, and be responsible for the chores in proportion to the hours he works. For example: if his dad works eighty percent of the time, and Trevor works ten percent of the time, then the domestic load should be split accordingly, meaning Trevor will be doing seventy percent more than his dad. Trevor could contribute to the cost of operating the car if he wishes to use it. If Trevor wants to go to university or any other kind of post secondary education, then his dad can support him as long as Trevor continues to pull his weight with the chores at home. Until Trevor experiences the responsibilities of living as an adult, he will never appreciate what his dad provides him. Another alternative is to have Trevor move out and support himself. This would be a wonderful way for Trevor to face the realities of life. Greg could implement this plan by setting a deadline for his son to find an appropriate job and a place to live. I would never suggest kicking a child out to the streets without a support system in place. Both Trevor and Greg should have a plan for living together and apart. It's important to always have choices.

The only way children can learn how to set boundaries is to experience them. That means it's up to us parents to lead by example. We do this by respecting ourselves by finding the balance between giving too much and not giving enough. Setting expectations and drawing a line with children also teaches them how to do this with love and respect. There is less chance of our feeling impatient, frustrated, and angry if we give our offspring reasonable boundaries. Of course, our children at times will not always like the boundaries we set and may not like us for setting them. They will come to appreciate these boundaries when they become parents themselves.

Balanced Lines = Balanced Children

Parents and their children are much happier when their home life is organized by setting boundaries. A structured environment with realistic guidelines helps children to understand their roles and responsibilities and cooperate as a family unit. It gives their lives balance and security.

Guidelines for children could include

bedtimes, getting up times, chores, education expectations, transportation, and social rules (friends, time to be home at night). Every family needs to set its own rules that work for them. There may be certain rules that are set in stone and others that allow for flexibility. Set rules and boundaries that work best for you and your family members and follow through with them.

Make a list of everything you need to support your family's routine

Do you need support or help from others outside the home to make your life work? Who will help? How much will it cost? Be creative in financing your needs; for example, when children are young and need a babysitter, trade hours of babysitting with another mom to avoid decreasing the cash flow. Teach older kids how to use the transit system or use a taxi service if you have to.

House Rules: Be clear with your children

Write out the house rules and post them so everyone knows the expectations. Also make it clear what the consequences will be for disobeying the rules because children will test you and try to push the limits. Be firm. Be flexible only when the situation absolutely calls for it. We cannot live so rigidly that there isn't any room for the exceptions. Allow your children some individuality. Let them have their way on the small stuff. For example, I didn't set any hairstyle rules when my children were growing up. They got to choose whatever style they wanted.

Working Together as a Team
A Game Plan for Couples

There is no one-size-fits-all prescription for building a married life that supports both partners. However, working together as team players with clear roles and responsibilities will give you a great foundation to support your individual and shared needs.

I strongly suggest that every newly married couple or a couple planning to live together decide who is going to do what in the business of a relationship. Who will be the breadwinner? Is it a joint venture? Is there a stay-at-home mom involved to raise the children? Who is going to do the dishes? Whose responsibility is it to change the diapers? Who's going to vacuum? Who will do the cooking? The grocery shopping? Who will mow the lawn? Who will shovel the driveway when it snows? Which partner will get to sleep while the other gets up to look after the children? Your whole list of responsibilities needs to be made clear before people start living together. If you are living with a partner and struggling with deciding who's responsible for doing what, then by all means sit down together and make your list. Do it now, before resentment builds up and poisons the relationship to the point of no return. Or you find yourselves making an appointment to visit a marriage counsellor.

What went wrong?

At the beginning of my marriage, my husband made a list of our responsibilities and roles in the relationship. Unfortunately, I didn't step up to the plate and tell him that I didn't agree with the assigned roles. For example, on my side of the sheet of paper, I was given one hundred percent responsibility for childcare, whereas I felt that a father should have at least ten percent responsibility since it gives him a chance to interact with his children. On his list was one hundred percent responsibility for handling the money in the marriage since he was the breadwinner. I wanted some say and responsibility concerning the budget, but I didn't speak up. Before long, it became an issue in our relationship. It took nineteen years for him to allow me to look after part of the budget. When that happened, our issues with money started to turn around. But by that point, I was resentful that my husband hadn't asked me what roles I wanted to play in the first place.

There's a huge difference between someone doing a list of chores or responsibilities because that person is willing to do it rather than feeling compelled to do it. The truth is that I had failed to speak out to make the arrangement fair to me. I had agreed to my husband's terms in order to please him and avoid conflict. He never forced me to agree to those terms. And I ended up feeling bitter because I had given away my power when it came to money. I recommend that couples make a financial plan together with their full consent since both parties are so deeply affected by it.

So the message here is for you to be clear and honest with yourself and your partner when writing up your list of responsibilities. What are you willing to do and what you are not willing to do? For your agreement to work, you must be able to draw the line and say "No" or "Yes". Otherwise, the price you'll pay is losing yourself in the process. When boundaries get eroded away in a relationship, we wake one day wondering who we are and what happened to our lives. The point is for you to agree to a list of roles and responsibilities with boundaries that seem fair. My idea of fair would be an agreement in which the needs of both of you are understood, respected, and met.

Money & Marriage
Taking Financial Responsibility

The way you handle money in your marital relationship can add stress to your life at work. You may allow your personal boundaries to be eroded by taking on too much work because you are in financial trouble at home and desperately need to keep your job. Taking financial responsibility and having sound money practices in the life you share with your spouse or partner will allow you to make better career decisions.

The place to begin working on your financial picture is at home. Many people end up divorced or very unhappy in their relationships over the issue of money. With our different personalities, upbringing, and values around money, no two people are going to be alike. Still, when you're sharing your life with another person there should be a basic plan in place for your joint finances. It would be wonderful if couples in their twenties or early thirties set up a financial plan with a budget that works towards their goals and if retirement was something everyone planned for early in life. Unfortunately, most couples don't think ahead and plan for their future. If you and your partner have not set up a budget that reflects your long-term goals, including a retirement and estate plan, I recommend you do so as soon as possible regardless of your age. Build a foundation for healthy money practices with a plan that enhances your relationship and supports your values. The boundaries that need to be set around money are straightforward: a plan, a budget, and follow-through to execute it. Make the time and effort to sit down with your spouse or significant other to establish a sound and jointly agreed upon financial plan. Less stress around the subject of money will translate into a happier relationship.

Tip for Couples

Here is a practice that worked well in my marriage. At the end of the month, after taking care of all of our budgetary needs, including saving for retirement, RESPs, car maintenance, rainy-day fund, vacation fund, etc., we equally shared the disposable income. We called it our allowance or play money. If we had $100 at the end of the month, our play money was $50 each. All the financial needs were met and if we had any extra, it was used for guilt free spending within our means. We each had our own credit cards, so those bills had to be paid from our play money. This system worked well for us as it made us accountable and responsible.

Setting Boundaries for Cell Phones

Our relationships have changed dramatically because of the

electronic devices and digital screens we constantly have in front of us. These rapid forms of communication have enhanced our relationships in many ways. Because of their convenience, cells phones have increased the amount of regular communication that goes on between partners, friends, and relatives. For parents with children, cell phones are great for coordinating their schedules with their children's activities and also help to give children more security. Text messaging between friends and couples enhances their emotional connection, assuming that the texting is not under the "conflict" heading. Venting and clearing the air is beneficial in relationships, but it's most valuable when done in person.

On the other hand, the constant texting that people do when in the presence of others diminishes the quality of their social interaction with "live" human beings. There needs to be social protocol for the "when and where" of cell phone usage. In your relationships, maybe you need to come to an agreement about where to draw the line. When the phone rings, do you feel compelled to answer it while in the middle of a conversation with someone else? It drives me crazy when people are never able to ignore the phone. Don't be a slave to the phone. It's there to serve you not you it. What is your protocol regarding phone usage? Where are your boundaries?

Don't keep the ringer turned on or answer the phone, look at text messages, respond to the beep signaling incoming email, or type a text or email message when in the middle of meal, a conversation, while sleeping, or in the middle of having sex with a partner. It's annoying and disrespectful of your partner's need for sleep when you disturb them with the beeps and pings of text messages and email from your electronic devices. Even if you turn off the sound, are you tempted to check your email and text messages during the night? Are you addicted to your cell phone? Where do you draw the line?

How can you live in the moment or be "present" when allowing yourself to be distracted and your thoughts going elsewhere? Do you have balance in your use of high-tech gadgets in your personal life? Do you put the presence of others before the lure of the screens?

Your Circle of Friends - Choose Them Wisely!

We need to establish close and dear friends in our lives to feel connected and have a sense of belonging and community. In *The Blue Zones: Lessons for Living Longer from the People Who've Lived the Longest*, author Dan Buettner shows through his research that friends, family, and community are a vital part of living a long and happy life. With our busy lives here in North America, many of us lose sight of these valuable connections. We get caught up in everyday life and are left feeling tired and drained to the point that our relationships suffer on every level. This is an area in our lives where there is an urgent need to set boundaries.

Men would benefit from a close circle of male friends for support and companionship that is unique to them. The same is true for women, although women tend to be more social to begin with and many women do have a supportive circle of friends. It's far less common for men to have that kind of support group. They usually prefer not to discuss emotional issues with their friends at the club or sports bar. If each partner in a married relationship has a close support circle of same-sex friends, I predict that there would be stronger relationships all around. Life can be challenging at the best of times, and having connections that help get us through these times helps to keep us grounded.

Can Men Be "Just Friends" with Women (and Vice Versa)?

Rarely. Men are programmed to be sexually attracted to the opposite sex. Women are programmed to be sexually attracted to men. Otherwise how would we populate the earth? The more time you spend with a person of the opposite sex and the more communication there is via emails, phone calls, text, messages, or Skype, the stronger the emotional connection will become. If you doubt this, look at situations of infidelity among your friends to see how these relationships got started and developed. Married men and women with emotional maturity know that to maintain a healthy level of intimacy in a marriage, they need to be best friends and remain so. Being emotionally intimate with someone else takes away from that bond in the marriage. That's why it is called "emotional infidelity". Close friendships with the opposite sex could lead to cheating on your spouse because the boundaries of friendship get muddy.

Setting Your Priorities

We only have so much time and energy in a day, week, month, and year. We cannot be everywhere and spend time with everyone whenever we like. Because of this, our relationships need to be prioritized. The people most important to you need your time and energy first. If you ignore your core people, eventually those relationships will crumble and fade away. Then you will have no core loved ones left to support you in your life. Chose carefully who you will make time for and draw firm boundaries to protect and nurture those relationships. Don't be sidetracked by the temptations of old flings, casual friends, or spending time in meaningless relationships. They will rob you of enhancing your intimacy with the people closest to you.

The following story illustrates what happens when someone shifts his whole focus onto spending time with friends and neglects his core relationships.

Paul's Story

Paul worked long hours in his career. His wife and children were in need of his presence and time. This was a point of ongoing contention with his family. One day Paul announced to his wife that he was going to go golfing once a week with his buddy Eric. She was furious. Normally she would have been supportive of Paul nurturing his friendships with his male buddies. The issue now was that it was at the expense of the time needed for her and the children.

Who comes first? Second? Third? Fourth? People need to be prioritized in a way that makes it possible for one's close relationships to remain close. Without time together, people drift apart, and sometimes so far apart that there's no coming back. The people who deserve to come first are those closest to you in your family unit. If those relationships are not being looked after first and foremost, it's not fair to go to the second tier of friends or family. If Paul had been spending adequate time with his wife and children, spending time with others would not be an issue.

Paul also found every opportunity to go out for dinner with his friends. Yet he would tell his wife that he had no time or energy to spend on a "date night" with her. He would go skiing with his ski friends, but never found time to ski with her. Whenever Paul got a social invitation from anyone, he always said, "Yes".

Paul needed to draw the line in the amount of time he spent with friends in order to put his family first and meet the needs of his wife and children. He had set no boundaries for the sake of his family's well being. There were no limits based on his sense of responsibility or desire to be with his family in response to his family's need for him. Family priorities simply didn't exist.

Deciding who gets first place, second place, and so on, on your list of priorities is a must when our lives are so busy and there is not time for everyone. Nurture the most important relationships first or they will die. What and who do you care about most? It will be reflected in the time you spend with them. Be clear about your choices and set boundaries to protect them from being compromised. Chose to live by intention rather than letting other people or circumstances sabotage your best interests. You can be the boss of your life by taking control of your time and keeping your goals and values thriving in your relationships.

When is it Time to End a Relationship?

When the pain of staying in a relationship is greater than the pain of leaving a relationship and all attempts to heal and repair have failed, then it may be time to let go and move on. Only you will know when you get to that point in your relationship. Make no mistake: it will be painful. The pull of the attachment strings in the brain is extremely powerful, which is what makes breaking up so difficult. Even when we know on a rational level that detaching from someone is the best thing for us, the emotional pain from this separation will persist until we have gone through the grieving process and healed.

Give yourself time to heal. If you have decided to end a relationship, honour your grieving process and allow yourself enough healing time. Do not expect to be "over" the loss of a loved one in a week or two. Take whatever time you need to feel whole and yourself again. How much time? There are no rules, so do not buy into set time limits. Everyone is different because of our unique brains, upbringing, or attitudes about life. The length and intensity of the past relationship comes into play, along with your level of determination to heal and move on.

The Power of Love Connections

When it comes to mending a broken heart, there are plenty of wishy-washy prescriptions in advice columns and self-help books. This advice often seems like it's based more on myth and fantasy than reality. Many people are not aware of the brain science that explains how our brain works in regard to love relationships. Scientists have discovered that the pain associated with loss and grieving is neurological and chemical. Your pain can be alleviated by making healthy changes in your behaviour, and not by popping pills. Here are some practical things you can do to speed up the healing process in your brain and heart that have worked for many people:

- Get some sun. Sunlight stimulates the pineal gland in the

brain. This helps to regulate your body's rhythms in a way that elevates your mood (Helen Fisher, *Why We Love*).

- Get regular exercise. There is much evidence to show the increase in dopamine, serotonin, endorphins, and other brain chemicals help elevate mood. Regular exercise can have as much effect on the brain as antidepressants.

- Cut off all forms of contact with your ex-partner. This will help you to detach emotionally and heal. If you share children, this suggestion needs to be modified for their sake. You may need to stay in contact to organize childcare and legalities. I also highly recommend that you keep things calm, respectful, and polite in front of the kids. Remember they are hurting too and probably more than you. It is our responsibility as parents to support and enhance our children's lives. Always consider their feelings in all your interactions with your ex partner.

- Talk to a professional who can offer support. Friends are great for venting, but sometimes a therapist can offer suggestions or insights that a friend cannot. Talking helps heal. Choose your listener with care.

- Take your mind off things by focusing on doing something that forces you to concentrate. Helen Fisher advises, "Do anything that forces you to concentrate your attention, particularly things that you do well" (*Why We Love*).

- Do not overeat or under eat. Go for the nutrients rather than quick fixes such as sugar, alcohol and drugs, which bring down your immune system.

- Follow a scheduled bedtime and wakeup time. This is to help regulate your sleep patterns, as these may be a challenge when fighting the blues.

- Instead of dwelling on the great memories and how wonderful your partner was, remind yourself of the bad times and their negative traits that bothered you. Make a list and read it whenever you start to think about how much you miss them. Carry the list with you.

- Stay busy.
- Do new things. Go out and join a new club, learn something new, interact with people, or take up a new sport. Our dopamine level (your body's natural feel good chemical) drops when we are depressed. "As you focus your attention and do novel things, you elevate this feel-good substance, boosting energy and hope" (Fisher, *Why We Love*).
- Make plans for the future. Write your plans down. Some people make a vision board to see the bright future ahead.
- Learn to meditate. Meditation has been recommended for relaxation and relieving symptoms of depression for a long time because it actually affects the brain and its functions.
- Try deep breathing techniques to help calm and relax you.
- Remember to be grateful for the goods things in your life.
- Put away reminders of the relationship such as photographs. If there are children involved remember to be considerate of their feelings. They may need pictures of their parents in their environment. Do not prevent or discourage your children from having a close and connected relationship with their other parent.

Doing the Work For Relationship Boundaries!

1. In the diagram below, write the names of the people who belong in the appropriate circles. The closer the circle is to you, the closer the relationship.
2. Then list challenges where the lines of these relationships are invaded and you need to set boundaries with these people or situations.

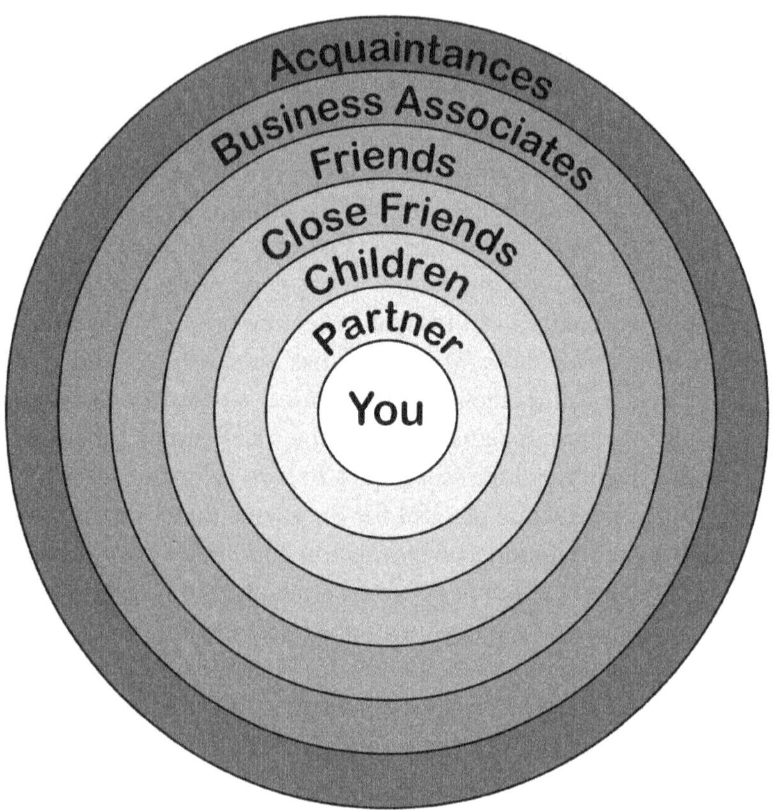

What Do You Really Want in Your Relationships?

Here's an exercise designed to help you know when and where to set boundaries in a relationship to make it work for you and your partner.

Establishing Relationship Boundaries

1. List your deal breakers for a relationship. Think carefully about all the things in your life that you believe in and live by. Here are some key areas to get you thinking: commitment to partner, business, children, eating habits, appearance, drugs, alcohol, smoking, exercise, religion,

spirituality, money, and sex. For example, financial responsibility is a deal breaker for me. If someone has not planned for retirement, has credit card debt, does not have a financial plan in place, and does not live within a budget, these are red flags for me and not someone I would consider dating or living with.

2. List the things that you are willing to compromise on in your relationships. Examples: food, how you travel, where you travel, how many children to have or not (maybe your child issue is a deal breaker or a surrender issue), appearance, sex (be clear what and how you will compromise on any topic under the heading of sex). Know when to compromise and when not to. Before saying "Yes" to everyone and anyone, consider the expectations, demands and requests being made. Are they reasonable and fair to you? Are they reasonable and fair to your partner? Are they things you want to do as opposed to what you have to do? (Of course there are responsibilities we have in life in order to reach our goals, whether in relationships or business.) Beyond this, are you experiencing a sick feeling in the pit of your stomach or a feeling that "something isn't right here"? How far does your boundary stretch before it snaps and you have given too much and lost yourself? Are you clear on when and where flexibility is appropriate?

3. List the issues (that you're aware of so far) that you can surrender on without surrendering yourself. For example: If where to travel on vacation is a 3/10 importance to me but it is a 9/10 importance to my partner, then I can easily surrender to that point. If I had a partner who loved to go dancing and it was a 9/10 importance to him and a 1/10 importance to me, I am willing to surrender and go dancing with him.

4. List the positives you are getting out of your relationship.

5. List the negatives in your relationship.

6. Rate on a scale of 1-10 how important each point is for both questions.
7. Overall, on a scale of 1- 10 how happy are you in your relationship?
8. Are you willing to pay the price of the negative for what you are getting under the heading of the positive? For example, if you are not respected and cherished, is this an acceptable price to pay for the positive that you are getting from the relationship (whatever that may be)?

Conclusion

Choose to design how your relationship with a partner will look rather than waltzing carelessly through life without any boundaries. Without being clear about your boundaries, it's all too easy to lose yourself and wake up wondering who you are and why you are in a relationship with someone. Come up with a plan for handling relationship issues to set a foundation for success with your partner. When you are clear about your boundaries, it will help to get you through times of conflict or indecision. Understanding what you want in your relationship will set the stage for real intimacy and a wonderful sex life.

Chapter 4
Intimate Connections - Raising the Blinds and Drawing the Lines

Revisit, re-clarify and recommit to what your soul desires.
Susan Scott

We talk about the importance of having healthy bodies, eating healthy food, and getting healthy by balancing everything in our lives. But there's not much discussion about the importance of having healthy sex lives and relationships. That topic gets put behind a door marked, "Private Keep Out". It's ironic that people feel inhibited about talking about their sexual desires and appetites when there's so much sex in the media. Many people don't know where to put boundaries in a respectful way in their relationships because of all the mixed messages we get about sex. The messages ingrained in you by society and your upbringing may have given you boundaries that you'd like to change.

Sexual intimacy with a partner can be extremely pleasurable, and it can give you a powerful bonding experience. It can be a means of answering your emotional as well as physical hormonal needs. Sexual expression can give you a healing experience if that's what you want. It also can cause a lot of confusion between people in relationships. When two people share a sexually intimate experience, they become vulnerable physically and emotionally. It's risky.

How vulnerable are you in your relationship with your significant other? How intimately do you really want to be known by your partner? Is sex just another physical need like eating or sleeping that you have to address? How important is sex in your intimate relationship?

These are some of the questions we'll explore in this chapter. While you may not agree with the positions I take on sexual relationships, I hope that the information and stories I share help you to identify what you want so you can decide what's right for you.

When to Say, "Yes" or "No" and Why?
Fear at the Core of Relationships

The challenge facing many women in their relationships with husbands or partners (though men face this, too) is how to say "No!" to having sexual relations with a partner, rather than saying, "Yes" most of the time. Women in our society were brought up in a belief system where traditionally women who said "No" could expect to be punished with husbands who cheated on them. Having an unwilling wife gave them the right to look elsewhere. Things have lightened up a lot since the 1960s as far as women's roles and rights in marital relationships are concerned. But a lot of women today still fear that they will be punished or that there will be serious, even dangerous, consequences if they do not participate in sex with their partner. That old meme "love, honour, and obey" still gets in the way when a woman and man form a committed relationship. Feeling duty-bound to "please your partner" diminishes rather than enhances a relationship. For most women, applying some common sense, self-respecting boundaries and initiating dialogue with her partner would be all that's needed to improve the relationship. But taking those steps is impossible until the underlying fear is dealt with. There is a deep trust issue at the core of most relationships that has been passed down through the generations.

Rejection Hurts - How to Say, "No!"

If you say, "No" to your partner, it could be interpreted as rejection and trigger feelings of inadequacy. My experience of being told "No" definitely left me feeling inadequate, undesirable, and unwanted. So you need to put a positive spin on things. The boundaries that you set around sex need to be framed in a way that doesn't rule out sex or show complete disinterest. For example, you might say, "Honey I know you really want me tonight but I am so tired that I just want to sleep. Could we set the alarm for a half hour earlier tomorrow morning and have sex then?" (Make sure you follow through with your promises or your credibility will be gone. Once it's gone, it is difficult to get it back.) Or in a case where the woman feels sexual desire but her partner is flagging, she might say, "I know you're not in the mood dear, but could you pop a Viagra to help *me* out tonight?" Men: The price of Viagra is cheap compared to a divorce.

Taking this cooperative approach in your sexual relationship goes back to the concept of "willing" versus "have to". Don't bother participating in sex if it's a "have to". If either partner feels they "have to" perform in the bedroom, it is time to deal with the underlying issues. Set some boundaries here and say, "No!" to an unsatisfying sex life.

Saying "No" because you have the flu or had three hours sleep the previous night is understandable. Saying "No" for weeks, months, or years is not acceptable and a red flag indicating more serious issues. But always saying, "Yes," at times when you sincerely need to set a boundary, is dysfunctional.

Say, "Yes" for the Right Reasons

Saying Yes to sex is wonderful if it's said for the right reasons. Those reasons should be right for you and your partner. Saying, "Yes" because you genuinely lust after and love your partner enhances your relationship. Decide where your desires and heart are. Set boundaries that reflect what you really want while still honouring your partner. Communicate your feelings openly and design your sexual boundaries together when possible and appropriate. Do not agree to anything that hurts you emotionally or physically. Do not agree to anything that diminishes your core beliefs or depletes your soul.

Sex as a Solution

Using sex to soften a conflict can be a good thing only if the conflict is not swept under the carpet. The issues outside the bedroom need to be addressed. Great sex does not translate into a great relationship and can actually be a form of denial about the real state of the relationship. Even though I addressed the issues that troubled my marriage by talking with my husband, our issues were never resolved, and my attempts to resolve them with sexual intimacy failed miserably.

Sex as Power Play

When sexuality is used as a form of manipulation and control in a relationship, neither person can be happy or fulfilled. This kind of behaviour points to self-esteem issues, sexual problems, and the inability to have a mature relationship with a partner. Generally there is poor communication between the partners. The following story about Ian and his wife illustrates how one partner attempts to manipulate the other in a battle for control and power – to no avail.

Ian and Sarah

Ian thought that if he appeased his wife by going overboard to please her every whim that he would get sex in return. This situation has many layers of complexity. The first issue is about withholding sex in order to control or manipulate someone else's behaviour. Women have a fierce reputation for doing this, although men do it too. This is game playing and it's great for building resentment, not for encouraging love and the connection that bonds couples. It implies that a woman has no libido of her own, that she is only going through the motions of the sexual act to reward the man (with the big libido) because he has been a good boy. Or that she can only have sex if he gets her in the mood (as if she has no responsibility for her mood) and that means obeying her every whim and command. If sex is used as a weapon, it is not a love relationship. If sex is withheld to manipulate, then the person withholding also loses out on having their sexual needs met. This is a "lose, lose" situation.

What does it say about a person's emotional maturity if they're using sex to control someone? Why would anyone want to be with a partner that could be controlled, not only in that way, but in any way? Why would anyone want to be with a partner that is playing the controlling game? This is a game that requires two people to play.

If someone isn't getting what they want in a conflict, learning to set healthy, respectful boundaries that apply to that situation and not the bedroom would be much more beneficial to all. If the conflict is so intense that the desire for sex is gone then that needs to be talked about, not ignored. If unresolved conflicts become ignored for weeks, months, and years then resentment rules the relationship and it needs help. Not wanting to cause conflict or "rock the boat" in order to get sex is not a relationship that is open for discussion on the real issues. Being in denial can prolong unresolved conflicts, and that makes a fertile breeding ground for greater resentment and contempt.

Ian did not want to give his wife Sarah an excuse to say "No" by disobeying her. The truth was that no matter how compliant Ian was or how "nice" he was or how much of a people pleaser he was, his wife would find a way out of having sex with him. The question is, why didn't Sarah want to have sex with him? Is it because of unresolved issues outside or inside the bedroom? Is it because she has a low libido and if so, why isn't she addressing that by getting some medical advice on the issue? If she has a low libido, that whole subject needs exploring. The couple needs to be honest and open so that the relationship as well as each individual can grow. Not being open and honest with yourself and your partner stunts growth.

Drawing the line

Ian could have set a boundary and said, "No, I will not avoid conflict. I will not be your puppet. I will not play this game." Ian's sexual needs were not being addressed and this conversation needed to happen with his wife. It is not okay to go through life without this basic human need for sexual intimacy being answered in a relationship if it is important to you.

What can we learn from Ian's story?
Risk conflict to resolve an issue

Many would prefer to avoid conflict because conflict is uncomfortable and potentially risky. But if the issue is not dealt with and worked through, guaranteed it will come back to haunt the relationship. Put on your "big boy or girl pants," and have the open and honest conversation that will reveal your true self and the source of the conflict. In other words, risk making your partner angry or actually hurting them. You cannot go around it, under it, or over it. You must *move through the conflict* to truly find resolution. Learn to say, "I am sorry." "I do love you." "I do want you." Talk it through. Maybe it can't get resolved in one night, but it's a start. Set a time when the conversation will be continued. Don't leave it hanging indefinitely. Find some kind of resolution within a designated number of days. Don't let it continue unresolved. Anticipated result: more emotional connection and sex with a willing and passionate partner.

What if you can't resolve the issue?
Seek professional help

People do get stuck. Many times it is possible to get un-stuck. Ask yourself if you feel genuinely motivated to make this work.

Would you be happier alone? Look at all possible scenarios. The solution may be that the relationship is never going to work and needs to end. Maybe brainstorming with your partner or a third party can bring about ideas you have not thought of. This helps you to see things differently and approach your relationship with a more positive hopeful attitude. This could open the door to greater intimacy in the relationship.

The Sexless Marriage

For many of you, it may be hard to imagine selling yourself out by staying in a sexless marriage unless it was necessary for medical reasons. Yet many couples, like Jack and Diane in the story that follows, do have this type of relationship.

Jack and Diane have been married for over twenty-two years. Jack will talk about his wife in the most positive way. He will tell you what a fabulous woman she is. Jack claims Diane has been his best friend and best support person when he has faced a number of crises over their years together. Diane is smart, slim, fit, and beautiful. What Jack will not talk about is that Diane has no sex drive. Jack would love to have a regular sex life with her, but she is not interested.

Jack is now in his fifties and exasperated over the "no sex" issue. He finally decided not to go without sex anymore. He paid to have sex with a twenty-year-old woman and had a sex life for a year and a half. This came to an end because he was getting emotionally involved with the young woman. This, he said, was unacceptable because he really loved his wife. It's only a matter of time before Jack finds someone else to have sex with again, other than Diane.

Drawing the line

I would challenge Jack on his meaning of love. It would be beneficial if partners could come up with an agreed definition of love and how that will be expressed in their relationship. If he really respected and cared about his wife, then she should have the freedom to decide whether or not she would like to stay with him under these circumstances. Or if he could not bear to hurt her in this regard, then ending the relationship may be an alternative.

Giving her a chance to participate

Jack could explain to Diane that a sexless marriage is unacceptable to him. Jack does have a libido and would like to share it with her. If she chooses not to have sex with him, then she should be informed that he'll have sex with other partners. Diane can stay in the marriage knowing her husband is getting his sexual needs met elsewhere. Or she can chose to leave the marriage if this arrangement does not work for her.

What could be done to improve Diane's libido? Why doesn't she have a desire for sex? Can this be fixed? Does she have a desire to fix the problem? If she is unwilling to address the issue, then Jack will have to decide for himself what he needs to do in order to be happy. It's important for Diane to understand that masturbation for Jack is not a substitute for a sexual partner. Sexual needs and desires go beyond the orgasm. The satisfaction from being touched, kissed, and fondled in the sexual act should not be underestimated. Masturbation is a temporary solution and does not satisfy the need for greater intimacy and a real partner.

Many people like Jack who are living in sexless marriages are not leading a life without any sexual fulfillment. If both parties are in agreement to this open lifestyle, then it's doable. If both parties are not in agreement to having sexual needs met outside the relationship, then this may require finding resolution of another kind.

Pre-Nup for Your Sex Life?

Setting boundaries around your sex life is necessary in any committed relationship. Ideally it would be best if these discussions happened before the couple made a commitment. Yet, even if agreements are made, new situations and issues will come up in life, and discussions will have to be initiated to resolve issues whenever necessary to keep both partners happy.

In our society people usually assume that women have a lower libido than men. The concept of libido, especially high libido, is associated with men. Men decline sexual activity due to lack of interest too, but that scenario is kept quiet, just like we don't hear as much about women with a strong sex drive. In any case, the issue here is about handling the difference in sex drives. If one person's libido is much stronger than the other's, it's important to come up with a plan for how that situation is going to be addressed.

For example, if one person's sexual desire could be described as fifteen percent and the partner's as ninety-five percent, how is the compromise going to happen? Is the gap an irreconcilable difference? If the gap is the space between fifty-five and seventy-five percent, compromises may be much more attainable. Is this a conversation that you need to have with your partner? What's stopping you?

Masturbation will only go so far. If you are in a monogamous relationship, are the rules going to change so the person with the higher libido can have sex outside the relationship? Or are you going to step up to the plate and participate? Don't fool yourself into thinking you can have a "no sex" relationship and your partner will never cheat on you. How long could you go without water? Food? Though sexual gratification is not a basic human need of that scale (you won't die without it), it's a basic need that can cause a person to suffer if not expressed. If you are a person who needs more sex in your life, set some boundaries with your partner. If you are a person who needs less sex, even more important to have this discussion around what boundaries will work for both of you.

Setting Boundaries in a Monogamous Relationship

To have a happy and fulfilling relationship with a partner, you both need to be clear about what you consider acceptable when it comes to spending time with others of the opposite sex and you'll want to be up front about situations that present themselves along the way. Otherwise, you'll run into trouble. The following stories show how boundaries can get crossed when expectations and communications are muddy for couples in monogamous relationships.

The "Innocent" Flirtation

Mark and Sarah are very social couple. They do many activities together with their friends. Sarah is an attractive female who gets male attention very easily. She engages men with flirting, touching (rubbing their backs or shoulders … so innocently?) and sexual innuendo. Sarah has male friends that she calls on regularly to chat with. Her male friends will invite them out to social occasions, but they only call and engage in conversation with her. When out socially, Mark is left out and feels like a third wheel in spite of his attempts to be included. Mark feels her behaviour is inappropriate for a monogamous relationship with him. He suspects she may have cheated on him at least once. He is tired and angry about all the attention other men get from his wife. When Mark has reached out to Sarah to talk through this situation, she takes no responsibility and accuses him of being jealous, insecure, and suffering from low self-esteem.

Mark is being the doormat. Sarah walks all over him. Mark hasn't set any boundaries for himself that would not tolerate being treated this way. This may be a case of low self-esteem but not the way Sarah sees it. People with strong self-esteem will attempt to resolve issues that diminish their souls. If they cannot, they will have the strength to draw a line and leave a situation that hurts them. What would you do in Mark's situation?

There could be a list of other possibilities of why Sarah

behaves the way she does. Mark and Sarah need help in sorting out their own individual issues and then their relationship issues. Both have to be willing to do the work. There may be issues from childhood that need recognition and healing, or issues in their present relationship that need addressing and healing. Either way, when ready, take action, and do the work to become healed, whole, and self-aware.

The Christmas Party - Where's My Date?

Doug and Laura, both in their fifties, were at the annual Christmas party for the company Doug worked for. The couple had been married for 14 years and had attended the party for eight and they knew most everyone. Laura spent the evening socializing with people other than Doug because he was engaged in talking with all the youngest and most beautiful women in the room. Doug didn't bother spending much time with any of the men, nor did he stand beside his wife or speak to her the whole evening. Laura was hurt and humiliated by her man's behaviour even though she had learned to expect this from him. When Laura complained about it to Doug after the party, he accused her of being jealous and controlling.

Men

If you feel the above behaviour is acceptable in a loving, monogamous relationship, please get out of that relationship. It is disrespectful and demeaning to your woman, and it makes you look insecure and immature. Stop making accusations of jealously and look in the mirror at what you are doing to bring on those feelings in your partner. Take responsibility for your bad behaviour. Obviously, you have not learned to think with the head on your shoulders. If you don't want any boundaries, then it is best that you remain single. No matter what kind of relationship you embrace, there will be boundaries of some kind on both sides of the relationship. I would suggest some self-growth work. Be clear on who you are and what you want. Then your behaviour should reflect your true self and your true values.

Women

Take responsibility for your life and relationship. If your man does not **want** to (versus **have** to) treat you with dignity and respect and behave like he cherishes you, consider the "why". A journey of healing old wounds may be necessary for each of you individually and then together. This journey could lead to a healed relationship or to the end of one. Either way is a better outcome than stagnating and being unhappy.

The Casual Coffee Date

Jim was a married man who claimed to be very committed to his wife, and yet he was regularly going out for coffee dates with other women. Not just any women, only women who sexually turned him on. Typically, these coffee dates would last a couple of hours. One day while out with a "lady friend," his wife calls him on the cell phone. He excuses himself to answer the phone. He does not tell his wife who he is with or what is he is doing. Jim says that he is in a "meeting". If this meeting is innocent and he's truly just spending time with a friend, then why is he lying? Jim is obviously feeling guilty because he knows this is not a situation that will foster an intimate relationship with his wife. Jim is not telling his wife because it would cause conflict.

Women usually know when other women are not a threat to their relationship and when they are. Men who spend time with other women they are sexually attracted to is putting themselves in a dangerous situation if and only if, they truly want to keep their monogamous relationship. (This example could have just as easily been made with the wife in Jim's position.)

Drawing the line

Jim has drawn a line with his wife, but is it a wise one? He has decided that he will lie about his situation rather than deal with the conflict with his wife. Jim gets points for boundary setting, but loses more than points for his lack of honesty, openness, and integrity. How long do you think this marriage will last?

The women Jim meets secretly are also responsible for setting boundaries. Clearly many women do not care if they entice a married man into having an affair. Some believe they can steal the man away from his wife with this strategy and many succeed. It often happens that these women are with someone who probably will leave them, also, for another younger and more beautiful woman. Forget about trustworthiness with either the man or the woman in this scenario. There are plenty of women who will say "No" to the coffee dates, touching, innuendos or anything else from married men that is not appropriate and invites an affair.

Sometimes women who entice married men do so because their needs are not being met in their own marriages. Maybe these women are in need of some love and attention and will take it anywhere they can get it. The place to look to find out the reason for what's happening with such relationships is at home.

Old Flames Can Spark Trouble

Some people manage to keep up a strong friendship with a former girlfriend or boyfriend long after breaking up with that person and marrying someone else. But that's rare. Most of us find the need to sever those kinds of connections for the sake of nurturing our married relationship.

Rob, Carol, and Sandy

Rob and Sandy had a platonic relationship in their twenties. A few years later, Rob married Carol. Sandy has been pursing Rob ever since Rob and Carol got engaged. Sandy asked Rob why he was marrying Carol when he should have been marrying her. This was Sandy's theme and intention for twenty-five years. Sandy made it clear she wanted Rob to be more than a "friend". She wanted him as a lover and her mate. Over the years, Rob and Sandy kept in touch by phone and email, met for coffee, lunch, or dinner many times – all of which Rob paid for. Rob would also go and pick Sandy up for their "dates". Then, Facebook came along, and of course they shared their lives on Facebook as well. Ninety-nine percent of the interaction between Rob and Sandy was done behind Carol's back. Rob went out of his way not to tell Carol the truth. This deception went on for years. When Rob finally did divulge the truth about Sandy, Carol was devastated. At one point, Rob told Carol he would not "see" Sandy anymore. Carol assumed this meant he would not be in contact with her in any way and would completely end the inappropriate relationship. Two years later, Carol found out this was not the case. The two of them were still emailing and calling each other. This play of words on Rob's part was deception at its best. Rob was not turning out to be a man of honour and integrity. His credibility was damaged and his trustworthiness diminished.

Rob claimed that he had no interest in having a romantic relationship with Sandy even if he was single. Rob felt she was not his type. Yet he continued to lead her on and not draw a line with her. Rob did not want to "hurt" her feelings. What he did was to hurt her much more by misleading her with his actions. Also, Rob chose to hurt his marriage and his wife's feelings. Where are Rob's priorities? If he cares so much about the old girlfriend and her feelings, then he should leave his wife and be with this other woman. But Rob insisted that was not what he wanted.

Here is a case of emotional infidelity. Rob was not emotionally committed to his marriage. His heart was not fully present. He was not ready to get married those many years ago when he could not set a boundary with his old girlfriend. His priorities were not in alignment with a commitment to his marriage. His best friend was not his wife. Men, if your wife is not your best female friend, that will cause a huge disconnect. Fix it now. Get help – or end it.

Sandy had no boundaries about pursuing married men. She was also obsessed about Rob. What does this say about her? What happened to the concept of healing and moving on from a broken relationship?

What about Carol's boundaries? She should have set a boundary about having an old girlfriend in her marriage right from the beginning when they were engaged. Carol knew about the phone call that Sandy made before they were married because Carol was standing right beside Rob when it happened. This was Carol's opportunity to ask Rob if he was willing to give up his old girlfriend. If he was not, Carol should have ended the relationship then. Unfortunately, Carol did not have the foresight and maturity at the time to do so. Carol chose to believe Rob that they were only "friends". The red flag was that Sandy's message (in the phone call) made it clear that her intention with Rob was not "just friends".

To Be or Not To Be Committed

This was a cluster-case study to illustrate situations where couples in committed relationships were not willing to set boundaries. In the end, each situation contributed to the demise of the marriage. When a partner in a relationship finds the need to be emotionally and or sexually validated by other people outside the relationship, that person is usually very insecure and has low self-esteem. It can be a sign that there is a huge disconnection or dysfunction in the relationship. For example, one or both partners may not feel loved, respected, and cherished. Or maybe one partner has so much testosterone (could be male or female) that committing to a monogamous relationship will never work for that person. It could be that a person's brain type, personality, and or environmental influences (peer pressure) are such that being in a committed relationship is not appropriate for that person. There are many factors to consider beyond these obvious scenarios since there are endless reasons why people do the things they do.

Secrets: Lies by Omission

Good marriages and lasting partnerships are based on trust and honesty. The willingness to be open and vulnerable allows one to be truly known and creates intimacy. The following story shows what happens when one partner in a married relationship conceals the truth to avoid the consequences.

Bruce and Barb

Bruce regularly phones Barb to let her know he will be home late from work because he is going out for drinks with his colleagues. What he doesn't say is that all his "colleagues" are single, good-looking women that he is sexually attracted to. Nor does he mention the flirting, sexual innuendos, dancing, or the list of other secrets he keeps from his wife, such as getting stoned, hiding money, cruising the porn sites, and making coffee dates with women he wants to seduce. (We can all make a list of our own secrets I am sure. I don't want to leave out the fact that the story could have been turned around to make Barb the one with secrets.) Bruce leaves out this information because he knows it would cause conflict with his wife. Barb is no dummy and would call him on his pre-affair behaviour, among a list of other issues. This would open the door to conflict and eventually lead to uncovering the real issues of their broken marriage.

Bruce has taken the attitude of "what she doesn't know won't hurt her". What he does not realize is that this approach is really backfiring. What she doesn't know will hurt him. He will never be really be known by her and what issues he is truly dealing with. Emotional connection and intimacy will never happen for him because these things often occur in the face of conflict and misery, not just the easy, happy times. Bruce has built a wall around himself that only he can decide to tear down. He made a choice not to be known by his wife. He feared that if Barb knew how unhappy he was and where his infidelity might be leading, she would leave him. This makes him extremely vulnerable. Yet, if their relationship is such that he cannot be himself and be open about who he is, maybe being single again is the best thing for Bruce. Then he wouldn't have to pretend to be someone he is not. Bruce could live a life being authentic and true to himself. I will also point out, from my personal experience, that pretending or trying to be someone other than yourself is extremely stressful and wears greatly on your health.

Let's turn that around and look at the situation from Barb's perspective. She is not aware of the real person she has devoted her time and energy to and this is a huge betrayal issue. Bruce robs her of the opportunity of choice. If she knew the truth, she could choose to leave and be with someone who is not pretending. That way, she'd have the opportunity for a truly intimate, emotionally connected relationship. Without Bruce being honest and open, Barb will never be able to get what she desires and deserves. So what she doesn't know, does hurt her and steals her chance of ever having what she really wants. What gives Bruce the right to take this opportunity away from her?

When listening to the stories of my clients during our sessions, the excuse I hear over and over and over again, from both sexes, is that they are not up front about issues because they know it will cause conflict: "He (or she) will be really angry, upset, and will criticize me." "I do not feel our relationship is a safe place to bare my soul and confess my sins." To this I say, "You are right!" The reaction you get will probably not be a pleasant one. But that is not a reason to lie about who you are. Take a deep breath and prepare to deal with the negative reactions. Don't expect to be treated like a Prince or Princess from a Walt Disney movie when you are the one causing the pain. Take all due responsibility. It is unfair to expect your partner to be calm and pleasant when you have hurt them. Yes, your partner may lash out. Sooner or later – probably later, when things have calmed down, the real conversation will take place. Maybe a counselor will be necessary to referee.

When we are hurt, we feel the need to express our pain. However, there's a difference between going ballistic and expressing our pain in an acceptable way and it's important to draw the line. Going into a rage or being out of control is not acceptable behaviour no matter how greatly you may feel you have been wronged. On the other hand, I do believe that the person who is hurting has the right to express his or her feelings. Why should a person have to suppress feelings in order for someone else to speak? Why should only one person be allowed to express themselves truthfully and not the other? That is assuming that both parties are mature, emotionally stable adults.

The more secrets you have, the less known you are. Is this what you want? Ask your partner if this is what he or she wants. If you speak openly and honestly and both agree to honour each other's boundaries, then your relationship will most likely work, since you are being true to yourself and your partner.

Finding Emotional Connection
Stepping Naked into the Light

You will never grow to a place of true intimacy with another human being without being honest and open. To be truly loved and accepted, your partner needs to know you. That's the scary part: becoming vulnerable! When you allow someone to see the real you, there's always the risk of being rejected. There are also great rewards in allowing yourself to be loved and accepted as you are. You will never know the joys of being "known" without taking the risk of being hurt. Embracing your vulnerability is an important step.

If you are with a partner that you don't feel you can be honest with, then you have some choices. Change the relationship by changing your level of openness and vulnerability. Get professional help to get through conflict caused by this transition if need be. Again, maybe stepping up to the plate will end the relationship, but not being true to yourself won't create a real relationship anyway. You also have the choice of remaining in a partnership where you are not open and honest for your own reasons.

Remember that you're not being true to yourself if you compromise yourself too far. For example, I started out my marriage with the values of openness and honesty, but after years of unresolved conflicts and hurt, I gave up on this. I became closed and emotionally withdrew. In the end, I hurt myself the most. I needed to end the relationship to find myself and go back to the values I most wanted to express in a relationship. In order to do this, I had to live these values, which meant leaving my husband.

This course of action worked for me, but I'm not suggesting for you to give up on your own relationship. I know couples that did learn how to be open, vulnerable, and true to themselves. They worked through this journey together and came out on the other end in a happy and fulfilled relationship. Their values and beliefs were close enough in alignment that the success of the relationship was possible. Acceptance can happen if one or the other person does not have to compromise on core values.

Taking Risks
Allowing Yourself to Be Known

How much of yourself are you willing to expose? How vulnerable are you willing to be? How "known" do you want to be? By whom?

Enduring Relationships & True Intimacy versus
A Quick Fix & Fantasy Playmate

After we get beyond the infatuation stage and past the

"honeymoon," maintaining a real and satisfying relationship, inside the bedroom and out, takes time, effort, and energy. Are you up for the challenge? Are you truly committed to the task? Consider how you feel about the following topics.

Pornography

Some people have boundary issues with online pornography because it's replacing real life sexual relationships and true intimacy with the simulated sex on porn sites. Are you spending your sexual energy on the porn sites instead of using that energy with your partner? Is the time you spend in your "real-life" sex life diminishing because you are having your orgasms in front of a screen instead of in bed with someone real? Is it your intention to create distance from your mate and withdraw from your sex life with them? Some women with a libido may feel cheated in their sex life if their partner isn't interested because he gets his needs met on the porn sites. Where are your priorities? Do you have any boundaries with pornography? Are you clear about your boundaries with your partner? Do you hide the truth? If so, why?

Casual Sex?

Then there are the online websites for prospective dating and or sex. Some married people cruise the dating sites to find sexual partners or make connections and fulfill needs that are not getting met at home by their partners. The sex sites are overflowing with married people who want more sex than they are getting or wanting at home. Is this where you want to be? Is this your answer to the problems you may be having at home? Are you living a lie? Is it okay with you if your spouse is getting their needs met from online sources?

Do what you feel is right for you

As long as you are honest and don't hurt anyone else emotionally or physically, and your partners are consenting adults, you are free to choose your sexual relationships and adventures. However, sex can be complicated, because getting involved with a person sexually is not a clear-cut experience separate from emotional and or physiological factors. Sometimes we may want it to be, as in a case where a man hires a prostitute to have his hormonal needs met. But even a "casual" encounter can have a huge ripple effect on the people involved. For example, why does a woman sell her body? What is going on in her life to be in this position? Would she rather not be? Why is the man paying for sex? Is this what he prefers? Or does he have emotional issues preventing him from connecting with a partner or vice versa?

Casual sex is sometimes used as an excuse for not getting into a serious relationship. People use it to get the validation they need from others without making a commitment to the relationship. Confusion, contradiction, and disconnect between behaviour and verbal assertion is common. For example, someone may claim that a sexual experience means nothing to them, and that it's "just for sex," when in reality that relationship is an attempt to find emotional connection. They may be feeling empty or lonely and looking to fill a void. Maybe they do know who they are and what they want, so casual sex seems to work for them. The trick is to find mates who are honestly on the same page. Many people struggle with knowing what they really want in a relationship. This is where having clarity on who you really are becomes important. Your lack of clarity and resulting behaviour can end up hurting you as well as other people.

As you can see, the subject of intimate relationships can become very complicated. Both mental and physical health issues may influence who you are sexually. Whatever you decide to do for your sex life, set clear boundaries for yourself and be clear about those boundaries with the people you choose to be sexually intimate with.

Health Issues Getting in the Way?

Sexual intimacy is important in one's love life. Giving physical expression to our feelings helps partners to bond at a deeper level. If you desire to have sexual relations with your partner but find that you can't "get it up," then your sex life may be in need of medical attention. If you experience low testosterone, estrogen issues, or any other kinds of hormonal issues, medical issues or prescription side effects that influence your sexuality, seek medical help. Do not settle for a poor sex life if there is something that can be done to enhance it. Take responsibility and don't make excuses. All too often, I have heard people say they're not up to having sex because of things that actually are in their control and changeable. If it is truly a situation that is not changeable, then be honest about that also. This is where it is vital to be partnered with your best friend that you share many things with outside the bedroom. Love has many expressions.

Dopamine & Novel Experiences
Fight the Boredom!

I love ice cream. Really I do. It's delicious and makes me feel happy while eating it. But if I ate ice cream every day of my life, it would become boring and undesirable (not to mention the weight I would gain). If I want to keep ice cream in my diet, (note I said "keep" not replace) then I need to find different and novel ways to approach it. I can choose different flavours, eat it in different places, have low-fat or high-fat varieties or mix ice cream in different foods such as baked goods or my morning shake. You can probably see where this is heading. Sex with your partner does not always have to be the same. With some forthright discussions, your desires and novel ideas can be integrated into your sex life as long as both parties are willing to experiment.

The importance of new and novel experiences to keep the sex drive alive cannot be underestimated. The information on brain science is now explaining why. Our brains get a boost of dopamine with new, different and unexpected moments or experiences. Variety is the key. When in a committed, long-term relationship, try out many exciting and novel experiences to get the dopamine boost. Make the effort to foster as many common interests as possible. Those common interests should include adventures or hobbies that excite both of you. Create a lifestyle of doing unusual things together. Plan for something "unexpected". A simple example of this is humour. It is unexpected and raises the dopamine in your brain. Remember how you feel when you are with someone that makes you laugh. Sharing humour is so important because of the triggers for dopamine. Sex increases testosterone, which also results in more dopamine. It would not be very stimulating or satisfying to be in a long-term relationship without sex, new experiences and a sense of humour.

Having time apart also translates into stimulating dopamine in the brain. When a reward is delayed, more dopamine is spread into the brain. So honour your time away from each other to reap the rewards. Making an effort to prevent boredom will pay off big in the long run.

Keep the Drive Alive

There are some standard practices that couples can use to increase the dopamine level in the brain and nurture their relationship. Here is a list of ideas to keep your relationship as well as your "drive" alive.

- Have mutual respect.
- Show appreciation and gratitude.
- Be committed.
- Listen.
- Foster and grow common interests.
- Spend time together.
- Spend time apart.
- Cherish each other.

- Maintain integrity.
- Accept imperfections.
- Forgive (when appropriate). Do not forget the lessons you learn. Do not carry grudges.
- Take care of your body, health, and grooming.
- Be trustworthy.
- Be open and honest.
- Please the other with acts of kindness and or service only if it is not eroding your own boundaries or compromising yourself.
- Fight fair: no name-calling; stay on topic (do not digress to other issues); do not criticize the other and be defensive if the issue is about you.
- Compromise when appropriate but do not erode or diminish your core values.
- Do not cheat on your partner.
- Do not lie to your partner even by omission.
- Be respectful of your boundaries as well as your partner's.
- Have a team attitude rather than be on opposing teams.
- "Choose your battles".
- Don't settle for a sexless relationship unless there are extenuating circumstances.
- Communicate your desires and needs. Remember your mate is not a mind reader.
- Ask questions instead of making assumptions.
- Show your love for your mate in their love language as well as yours.
- Be thoughtful and kind.
- Be your partner's best friend.
- Share novel experiences as part of your lifestyle.
- Do not play mind games, punish, or ignore your partner.
- Share food together.
- Play together.
- Do not use sex to control your partner's behaviour.

- Have fun with sex.
- Don't take sex too seriously. It's okay to have hormonally driven sex that's not a heavy emotional experience with your partner.

Conclusion

When it comes to the expression of your sexuality, there is no right or wrong way to go about it. Just be clear with your partner about your needs and desires. You may not be completely clear about who you are sexually and what you desire from an intimate partner. It may take some thinking outside the box and trying different things in order to find what works for you and your significant other. Letting yourself be known to your partner is vital for creating real intimacy between you. Being open and honest translates into being fair to the other person because you're not robbing your partner of choices by pretending to be someone you are not. Chose to live with intention by making conscious choices that bring fulfillment to your life. Know where your boundaries are and communicate those in your intimate relationships. Understand the difference between compromising and settling. Settling is a "lose–lose". Compromise is a "win–win". There's nothing in life that can beat this kind of "win – win"!

Chapter 5
Health - Your Body Knows Best!

*Would you prefer to continue limping
or are you ready to remove the stone from your shoe?*
Susan Scott

As I sat at my first breast cancer support group meeting, I didn't know if I was crying because of the diagnosis of breast cancer or the breakdown of my marriage. I was grieving for both at the same time. I felt betrayed by my body. How could this have happened to me; the nutrition expert and fitness queen? I worked out at the gym, cycled, or skied five or six times a week. My diet was about as good as it gets; organic whole foods, no alcohol or caffeine, anti-cancer supplements, and yet here I was with breast cancer. The journey that followed on my road back to health taught me that making those lifestyle choices was a good thing. My diagnosis could have been a lot worse had I not taken care of myself. However, not to underestimate the importance of taking care of oneself, there is more to cancer than lifestyle. Sometimes it's just dumb luck: the genes you're born with. Medical science has helped to explain the mysteries of our physical bodies and certain people are more prone to getting diseases such as cancer. Breakthroughs in science also show that stress compromises our immune system. My marriage no doubt contributed to the breakdown of my health. Years of living with unresolved issues in a chronic state of unhappiness can be very stressful to the body as well as the mind.

My cancer diagnosis was a big wake up call. It started me on my journey to find out what real health was all about. Besides undergoing radiation and surgery, I also explored some alternative healing therapies and read everything possible to get well. What I learned was that your body's health depends on setting boundaries in all areas of your life. (My biggest challenge was in the area of stress.) It's not enough to cut out smoking or lose 40 pounds or even to have a positive attitude, though all of those steps would help. We need to live on course with who we are combined with all the healthy lifestyle options in order to support a vibrant healthy body.

Dealing with Stress - Where's the Line between Enough and Too Much?

Those of us who survive a potentially fatal disease or illness are the lucky ones. Many people die a sudden death, maybe due to a fatal accident or a heart attack. These people don't get a second chance at anything in life because they are no longer with us. No last goodbyes, no opportunity to make a bucket list, let alone fulfill it. So if you're experiencing a lot of stress, you can be thankful for this wake up call that your body is giving you. I won't write pages about how bad stress is for your physical, mental, and emotional health. You already know this. But if stress is building up in your life and creating symptoms, it's important to check your boundary lines. Are you doing too much? How do you define what's too much for you in the important areas of your life? What are you doing to be successful at your job? How do you support your family members? Your friends? Does any of it feel like too much to handle? When you're living beyond your energy levels, it can't help but cause enormous stress in your body.

Many people have taken on too much responsibility in our society. We have been told we can do it all: have a career; be great moms and dads; have wonderful relationships; and pursue our own interests on the side. The expectations are so high that sooner or later we can crack and break down. The stress from your career alone can be overwhelming just as coming home to more stress can become unbearable. Dealing with a long list of responsibilities creates chronic stress and increases the possibility of a major health issue.

Let's get real here. We only have so much time in a day, a week, and a life. Maybe your long "to do" list will need to be shortened. To take care of your top priorities may require some sacrifices. Maybe our partners need to readjust their expectations of us. Chances are your partner is stressed and would like to make some life changes too. It's virtually impossible to be super domestic and super moms and dads while also being career driven and pursuing outside interests. It comes down to this: What is really important to you? How can you make your life work? To have a life that really serves you, boundaries need to be set with others. If we don't draw those lines, the expectations will drown us and the resentment can kill our relationships. Our true selves will be lost. The price will be our health and or our relationships.

Are You Ready to Change?

Most people don't think about changing an unhealthy lifestyle or pattern unless they're provoked by a health crisis in their lives or feel highly motivated by some other reason, such as getting in shape to attract a sexy mate. When I work with clients who wish to lose weight, my first session with them is all about motivation. Why do you want this goal? Is it your goal or a "should" recommended by someone else? One of my clients, whose doctor told him he needed to lose 60 pounds, was never motivated to do so because this was what the doctor wanted - not himself. Fifteen years later, the man is still 60 pounds overweight. He may never want to lose this weight. That is his choice. The question for you today is: Are you ready to set boundaries in your life to make the changes you want rather than what someone else wants you to do? To make a change in your life you need to be ready. It is not good enough just to say the words. Action must be behind the words. The time must be right for you. I encourage you to embrace this moment and declare, "Yes, my time is now!"

Work Less, Play More!

Whether we overwork ourselves because of the need to prove ourselves to the world, please other people, or for various other reasons, the effects of overwork will begin to surface in our lives. Chronic exhaustion shows up in a number of ways, including impatience, depression, lack of energy, insomnia, anger, inability to focus, and a general lack of enthusiasm for life. Some clients have shared with me their regret for missing out on more joy in their lives because of the excessive hours spent at work. Yet the pull to be successful in our careers can seem relentless.

To adjust the line between work and play is the challenge. Our health depends on this line being flexible enough to allow for de-stressing in whatever form works for you. Learn to incorporate downtime into your life. Give your body a chance to heal and recover from the stress it's experiencing. Do not turn 65 with regrets about not taking time out to relax and re-connect with yourself and loved ones. Finding the balance between work and play is much better than charging ahead and losing precious years of your life through health issues.

I deeply regret having allowed myself to become stressed to the point of exhaustion from trying to please others for so many years. My stress showed up as grumpiness, impatience, and a lack of energy to fully connect with my children and husband. If I could go back in time, this is something I would change. Less work, more play! Learning to forgive yourself and letting go of regret is a way to improve your health too. It's an important step in the growth process. Carrying the weight of regret can be stressful.

Communicate Your Needs to Others

In order to adjust, add, or change boundaries, communication with the people involved in your life needs to happen. If you wait for others to pick up on your dissatisfaction with a situation or hope they'll have the miraculous ability to read your mind, obviously nothing will change for you. It's your responsibility to communicate your needs in all situations.

Ed was a client of mine who was in desperate need of health and wellness guidance. He was experiencing painful, stiff joints and was diagnosed with arthritis. He was suffering from sleep deprivation, which only made the pain in his body worse, as he was tense all the time from stress. Ed's body was saying, "No!" but he was ignoring the message. Eight years later he was treated for prostate cancer. Ed feels that his life could have been different had he taken the initiative to communicate his needs to his business partner as well as his wife and three children.

Conversations around roles for each family member needed to happen to improve Ed's situation. Like Ed, I had not stepped up to the plate to ask for what I wanted and needed from the people in my life. I could have made different decisions for myself to decrease my workload. I needed to set boundaries, but did not. Even when we do ask for help from others, there is no guarantee that we will receive the help we need. We can only control our own actions and behaviours in any situation, not those of others.

Knowing that you need to do less and decrease stress is one thing. Deciding what you are willing to compromise on to make that happen is another. Tough choices will have to be made. Before you make these decisions, it is vital that you are clear on who you are and what you want. What makes you happy? Who and what do you want in you life? Refer to the reflection exercises in the second chapter to help you make changes so that when you do, you will be confident these decisions are right for you.

Take Action to De-Stress Yourself

List the things in your life that cause you stress of any kind. How could you do life differently? What's holding you back? What are your fears? What can you do to bring your stress levels down? Here are some popular stress reducers:

- Exercise
- Talking
- Outdoor activities
- Music
- Meditation
- Yoga
- Sleep
- Laughing
- Socializing with friends
- Joining a weight-loss group or fitness club
- A massage
- A hot bath
- Reading a book

Experience Joy!

With stress comes tension. With joy comes ease. Doing things that bring joy and happiness to you relieves your body of tension and stress. You feel uplifted and refreshed.

For years, I have hiked in wilderness areas with friends and gone swimming at the lakes we discover along the way. Whenever I find an opportunity to be alone during a hike, I go skinny-dipping. It's the most freeing and exhilarating sensation. I come out of the water feeling calm and excited to be alive. If you don't have something that uplifts you like this, find it. It may take some time and effort, but keep trying until you do.

Stay away from drugs and alcohol for de-stressing. Drugs get you high, and that takes away your pain and makes you feel temporarily happy. But then you crash and burn physically and sometimes emotionally, as well. The purpose of de-stressing activities is to bring you up, not bring you down.

Experiment with new activities and keep exploring until you find your ultimate de-stresser and joy maker. Don't live life without doing things that make your body feel good and give you joy!

Nutritional Boundaries

There are countless books available on nutrition and many different ways of eating as a lifestyle to promote health. It's up to you to find the way that works for your body. As a nutritionist, I recommend that my clients experiment to find what makes their body feel its best. We explore different diets and add foods that enhance mind and body function. My purpose here is not to recommend that you eat only this way or that way. I will simply give you some basics to get you started, and you can expand your research to discover what's best for you. Please don't believe everything you read about nutrition. Much of the information you'll find has not actually been confirmed by research (as pointed out in the first chapter on Experts).

What is Best for You to Eat?

After being educated in the traditional sense (Montana State University) and then exposed to the natural and holistic teachings of nutrition through being a client of a naturopathic doctor, I would say that both schools of thought offer valuable information, along with some "facts" that are more fantasy than truth. We've come a long way in our understanding of how the human body works in regards to nutrition. But there is so much that medical science has yet to learn about diet and health. Until some of the latest dietary theories are proven to be truly beneficial, I think it's important to use your best judgment based on what we do know for sure, rather than going to extremes and taking a risk with your health. How can you do things differently right now?

Tips for a Healthy Eating Lifestyle:

1. Don't follow the fads.

2. Eat and drink organic, which means avoiding additives and chemicals.
3. Eat low fat protein, whether you chose to be vegan, vegetarian, or a meat eater.
4. Eat a wide variety of vegetables and fruit and lots of them.
5. Avoid sugar, bad fats, trans fats, processed foods, and excessive amounts of caffeine.
6. Don't overeat. Cut calories but not to the extreme of becoming unhealthy.
7. Avoid drugs and alcohol.

The Roller Coaster

It's difficult to stick to your good intentions when your blood sugar level drops. The power of low blood sugar on your brain and mood can be extreme. From my own experience, I know that I need to eat every three hours. If I don't have a snack with some protein and healthy carbs, my patience completely disappears and I become the "Wicked Witch of the West". In order to communicate effectively, your brain must be in a calm state. You will absolutely sabotage any efforts to set boundaries with yourself or others and follow through on them if you are impatient, nauseated, weak, shaky, light-headed, craving carbohydrates, and seeing spots in your eyes. How can you think clearly or behave rationally when you're experiencing symptoms such as these?

How to Break the Cycle and Get Off the Roller Coaster!

Here are some other dietary recommendations that will help to stabilize your blood sugar so you won't experience crash-and-burn symptoms. These foods also will help your body to burn fat rather than store it:

• Think protein first, good fats second, and healthy carbs third.

- Make protein part of every meal or snack. Eat lean sources such as fish, poultry, eggs, raw nuts, and seeds.
- Make the healthy fats and oils part of your diet: avocado, nut seed oils, extra virgin olive oil, raw nuts, and seeds.
- Limit your carbs to healthy sources such as fresh or frozen fruit, whole grains, vegetables, and legumes (beans, lentils, soybeans, peas).
- Listen to your body to know when you need a snack or a meal.
- Don't skip meals. It will only encourage your body to store fat.

Beware of Fad Diets

Fad diets have been known to take the credit for improved health; however, valid information is often missing from the so-called studies that support these diets. For example, a person on one of these fad diets can become more health conscious by exercising more, not eating refined foods, eating fewer calories, or decreasing stress levels. How do you know that these factors were not the biggest contributor to the person's change of health rather than a particular diet?

Often, fad diets will include a few known facts about nutrition and then fill in the rest of the story with opinions or pseudoscience. Too many times, people will try these diets, lose weight, and feel great. Then credit is wrongly given to the new diet. The truth is, you will lose weight on most any diet because you have cut calories: hence, the weight loss. Also, you feel great because you have cut out junk foods that contain bad fats, sugar, and refined products. Of course, you're inclined to think that the new diet is the best thing ever; however, usually fad diets will hurt your body if followed for too long because they restrict your variety of foods to the extreme.

I am all for eliminating food groups that are not good for our health. However, be mindful of which nutrients you are taking out of your diet that you will need to replace in other ways. For example, dairy products can cause problems for hormonal reasons. The amount of fat and estrogen consumed in a diet can influence hormones both in women and men. Calcium can be supplemented from other sources. Just be sure to research those other alternative sources to be sure your calcium intake is not hit and miss. If you are on a vegan diet, then find out where your sources of protein are coming from and be sure to calculate the amounts so that you know you are getting enough of it.

Nutritional Boundaries in Your Relationships

Now here is a challenge that many of us face when sharing our life – and our dining table – with others. How can you stick to your own dietary choices and food preferences when someone else has very different tastes and eating habits?

If there is only one person in charge of the cooking and providing the meals, does that person cook two different meals or does the person not preparing the meal eat whatever is prepared? The problem is that the meal may not work for both people. If one person prefers low fat, low sugar, and lots of veggies, and the other prefers high fat and no veggies, then the couple will need to come up with a plan that satisfies both of them. Personal health issues may be influencing these choices. For example, if the person wanting a low-fat diet eats a high-fat diet, that may translate into being overweight and very unhealthy. With two people and two different ways of eating, it's difficult to prepare one common meal. Having enough time and energy to make two separate meals that would work for each person may not be a logical solution. Expectations around mealtime need conversations that will invite choices and compromises from both parties. Draw the line for what each person is willing to do in the kitchen, given time and energy constraints.

How Can You Make Everybody Happy?

Any option that includes a "we" requires a willingness on both sides to cooperate. If there is no willingness from another person, then it's up to you to determine what you're willing and able to do as far as preparing meals.

1. Order frozen meals from a catering company that uses food that meets your standards. For example: organic chicken, beef, veggies, no dairy, low fat.
2. Each of you cook your own meal at different times.
3. Take turns cooking for both of you.
4. Cook together but make your own meals.
5. Find recipes that can be simply modified to suit each of your tastes.
6. Meal planning could be a shared experience, not left up to one person.

If others are influencing your food choices; for example, others are doing the cooking and making your food choices for you, then your dietary boundaries will have to be addressed. If you are the cook for the family, have conversations around expectations, wants, and needs. Shared responsibilities for meals are highly recommended. Children need to learn to prepare meals also.

Exploring Your Food Boundaries: Make a Food Plan

Without a plan, execution of new dietary habits will fall to the "waist" side. Take some time to think about your goals and how you are going to achieve them.

1. Write out your food plan.
2. Make a list of times when you get pulled off the plan. For example: When he cooks for me. When I am running late and grab something at the coffee shop. When I am feeling

down, eating emotionally. When I am tired and need more sleep.

3. Plan ahead.
4. Make a backup plan. For example, when your time is limited and you are running late, have high protein, healthy fats, and carbs in your car and at your desk.

How to do things differently:

- Say, "No" to others offering food you do not want to consume.
- Say, "Yes" to healthy choices.
- Eat before you are starving.
- Go to bed earlier.
- Carry healthy snacks in your brief case or purse.
- Make a list of things to do in order to avoid emotional eating.

Exercise, Exercise, Exercise: Stress Busters

Do all three types of exercise: aerobic, strength training, and stretching. Aerobic increases your cardio. Strength training builds and maintains your muscles. Stretching keeps you flexible.

- **Aerobic**: Cardio = Sweat, five to six times a week for 30 minutes or more. No need to exercise for hours a day to be healthy. Overdoing it can be as bad as underdoing it.
- **Strength Training:** Two to three times a week. There are different ways to build and strengthen muscle other than just using weights. Yoga is wonderful for building muscle and stretching. Do your due diligence to find out which type of exercise is best for you to build muscle.
- **Stretching:** This is necessary for everyone at any age.

Make an Exercise Plan that Works for You

Whether you do research to design an exercise plan yourself or ask a personal trainer to help you, make goals and plans that work for you.

- Make a calendar of when and what type of exercise you are going to do.
- Set boundaries for your exercise by keeping a daily record to hold yourself accountable.
- When did your exercise time get washed away?
- Why didn't your exercise time happen?
- Who is involved with why you didn't exercise today? The "who" could be you or someone else.
- What needs to happen for your exercise plan to be executed? Do you need to say "No" to someone or something? Do you need to say "Yes" to someone or something? What's holding you back?

Get Your Zzzzzzzs

The importance of sleep on your mental and physical health is well researched and documented. Here is a list of some of the health issues resulting from a lack of sleep:

- Depression and mood swings
- Bad eating habits
- Weight gain or loss
- Problems concentrating
- Bad judgment
- Distorted perception
- Lower energy
- Lower sex drive

Sleep Facts

- Sleep enhances memory and learning. It's difficult to learn new information with inadequate sleep. It is necessary to get a great night's sleep after learning the new information in order to absorb and retain it.

- Our body's metabolism functions better with adequate sleep. Lack of sleep contributes to a host of health issues, an increase in appetite, and cravings for high carbohydrate and high fat foods.
- Lack of sleep in the workplace can show up in errors, lower productivity, accidents and or irritability, to name a few symptoms.
- Immune function is at risk with a lack of sleep, which contributes to any number of diseases, such as cardiovascular disease, obesity, diabetes and cancer.

People are playing games and being entertained on the Internet into the late hours of the night at the expense of their sleep. When you are running a sleep deficit for this reason, then the Internet becomes a liability in your life rather than an asset.

For you to be a productive, mentally stable, and physically capable human being, you must put your need for sleep ahead of your Internet wants. When your Internet obsessions take priority over your need for sleep, you will pay a high cost in all areas of your life – including your ability to establish healthy personal relationships. Life online can't give you emotionally connected relationships with people in the real world.

Setting Your Sleep Boundaries

Adequate sleep requires a routine of regular bedtimes and regular getting up times. Discipline is the key. Sleep boundaries are a priority for me. Are they for you? Here are some questions to help you evaluate any sleep challenges you may have in your life.

1. Do you have a sleeping partner who likes to read at bedtime and the light keeps you awake when you are ready to sleep?

2. Do you stay up too late at night to catch up on work? Watch TV? Read? Play or work on the computer?
3. Is your sleep being disturbed by noise?
4. Do you get up very early to work on a project or to take care of others needs? Could these things be scheduled at another time of day? Why not? Who says?
5. Do you turn off the cell phone at night? Do you hear the pings for every text and email for late night calls? Have you informed family and friends not to contact you except for a true emergency, and after a certain time of night; for example, at ten o'clock in the evening?
6. Make a list of ways that your sleep could be improved.
7. Who do you need to have a conversation with to make this happen?
8. What do you need to do to be committed to a regular bedtime? And a regular wake up time?
9. Do you have any fears around these questions or issues? What are they?

Respecting the Boundaries of Others

We all want to set our own boundaries and do what is best for us. Now let's see how we score on accepting and honouring the boundaries of other people.

Diet

Do you respect other people's boundaries around food? Do those who want to eat differently or follow a special diet feel sabotaged by what you provide or make for them if you are in that role? Do you honour other people's food choices even if you disagree with them?

Sleep

Do you honour the other person's need for sleep in your home or in your accommodations when away from home by being quiet and keeping the lights turned off? Do you text or phone people in the same room after their bedtime?

Exercise

Do you honour the other person's exercise needs? Are you supportive or are you negative?

De-stressing

Do you honour the other person's choices for de-stressing?

It's far easier to set good boundaries when we choose to have relationships with people who have similar values, beliefs, tastes, and health-related practices. If one person is vegan and the other believes in eating meat and plenty of it, the difference may wear on both of you over time. If one person believes in having wine every night for dinner and the other person never drinks alcohol, this could become a point of contention between you.

Conclusion

Nutrition, exercise, stress, and sleep are elements of our health that are necessary to feel alive and strong. Taking care of these basics means that you will need to be clear within yourself about what is best for you and not have those lines eroded away. Make a plan and stick with it. Remember to communicate your boundaries with firmness, respect, and integrity. Stay strong and feel empowered by how great you feel!

Chapter 6
Boundary Lessons for Entrepreneurs

Leadership is the capacity to translate vision into reality.
Warren Bennis

The most important leadership quality for the entrepreneur to maintain at all times is integrity. Running a business can present many unexpected and difficult challenges. For the entrepreneur to have the strength to do the right thing, even when the consequences can range anywhere from unpleasant to devastating, it takes a guarded boundary around integrity when making decisions.

Standing Strong through the Storm

It was four thirty in the morning. The house was quiet. I woke up with a start after being up most of the night with our baby. I was shocked to see my husband sitting at the edge of the bed, dressed, and ready for work. He explained to me in a devastated voice that he had a decision to make by eight o'clock that morning and the consequences would change our lives.

My husband told me that he had two choices. The first choice: He could cut a legal deal and save us from financial disaster, but his honour and integrity as a businessman would be lost. The second choice: He could cut an honourable deal with his integrity intact. The consequence of that choice would be to go into bankruptcy. My response, "Bankruptcy, I can deal with. A husband with a broken soul, I cannot. I vote for honour and integrity." With tears streaming down his face, he said, "Thank you" and left for his meeting. I knew that our material possessions could be replaced. But how we conduct ourselves in one moment can never be taken back. We only had this one chance to make a choice that would decide the direction of our life.

Later that day, my husband phoned with a list of things we had to do to prepare for bankruptcy. In the weeks that followed, I emotionally let go of our material possessions: the new house, the nice cars in the garage, and my dream lot in Whistler, British Columbia. I grocery shopped with a calculator in hand so I would not go one penny over the allotted food budget. I grew my hair long so there would be no haircut expenses. I only bought clothes for the kids and that was at garage sales.

These were the best days of our marriage. I felt so happy – so empowered! Because I knew for sure that we had done the right thing. He did "right" by his business and I did "right" by my man. How could life get any better?

In the eleventh hour of this storm, the fellow businessman that my husband met with on that fateful morning put the pieces of the puzzle together and figured out what kind of choice he had made. So this man went to his boss and they came up with an alternative plan that bought us another six months in business. With my husband's tenacity, that six months turned into eight months and that eight months turned into a year and that year turned into three years … until once again, we had a healthy company. But wait! This time it was a wealthy company. He had gone from 38 employees down to a skeleton staff of five, which included my husband. And we were making 15 times the amount of money.

Eighteen years ago, that husband and that wife, for richer or for poorer, stood tall and strong, knowing they had honoured the deepest part of themselves and each other.

What do I know for sure? A life of integrity begins with intention and that power of intention compounds daily, so doing the right thing does not happen not by chance. I am not saying that when we do the right thing it is a guarantee for a Walt Disney happy ending! I do believe, however, that by doing the right thing, we keep our inner soul intact. We can walk through life, knowing who we are and stand tall and strong.

Do you stand tall and strong?

Is "honour" a word you would use to describe yourself?

What else does it take to make someone successful as an entrepreneur? Countless self-help books and biographies have been written on the subject. Some say that an entrepreneur is born with the brain and personality to be driven to realize a big vision. Other authors show that to become a successful entrepreneur it takes not only unique talents and skills but also extensive knowledge of the business world. The truth is that there's no one-size-fits-all formula for success. Malcolm Gladwell, author of *Outliers: The Story of Success*, shows that success comes from a combination of many factors, such as the society or culture being ready, hard work, the number of hours put into perfecting a talent or skill, personality, propensity for the necessary skill, upbringing, and being in the right place at the right time. The Beatles, Bill Gates, and Oprah Winfrey are examples. No matter how different the owner or the business may be, there are leadership qualities that are important for entrepreneurial success: knowing yourself, being authentic, having a clear purpose, understanding your business, and setting boundaries that allow you to focus on your mission.

As someone who has served in various leadership roles, including running my own business for many years, I have experienced everything from people management problems to financial challenges. Besides having passion for the work you do, you need perseverance and tenacity to get you through the tough times in business. If you are just starting out, then it's worth your while to do your homework and learn as much as possible from those who have achieved success. In this chapter, we'll look at the important role that boundaries play in the personal and professional lives of entrepreneurs.

The Head or the Heart – Who's the Boss?

The reasons why people are motivated to join the entrepreneurial community are as diverse as the many individuals who make up this growing community. Is the entrepreneurial personality born or is it made? Is it the result of our environment or the brain we're born with? Or both? Could it be that brain type also is responsible for the drive and success of the entrepreneur? This is an interesting question, and no one knows the answer for sure. Let's look at the brain type theory.

Brain Types - Which is Your Strongest Side?

It is common knowledge that the right and left sides of the brain are responsible for different functions. Our right brain is associated with "heart". Right brain function makes it possible for us to experience feelings of love and have intuition. The right brain is our creative side. It takes all the information and puts it together in a way that gives us understanding and knowledge. Without the right brain, we could not communicate and connect emotionally with others. Interestingly, everyone's right brain can be developed or trained to become more creative. Not everyone is a "born" artist or a visionary thinker.

The left part of the brain is known as the "head" side. Left-brain function makes it possible for us to analyze information and problem solve; it's responsible for logic, memory, and language. Many careers fall into the left-brain domain and many people learn to operate from this place; for example, accountants, physicians, or lawyers. Yet research shows that only a small percentage of people have a dominant left-brain personality.

For centuries, our society has focused on being successful from the "head" side, the left-brain side that favours logic over intuition or "heart". We are learning that the most successful and happiest entrepreneurs have trained their brains to honour and use both sides of the brain. This is not always an easy task. At times, the left and right brain may be in conflict with one another.

Finding the balance, by learning to understand which part of the brain should win out in a particular moment or situation, takes practice and wisdom.

Honouring Your Gifts

Regardless of your brain type and or personality, it is important to recognize and honour who you are. The unique talents and skills that you bring to your business are what will make you successful and different from the competitors. Being true to yourself is what will bring you the greatest happiness.

When you're connected on a deep emotional level to your work, it's easy to get completely absorbed in it. Hours disappear when you're intimately focused on something that satisfies the soul. It feels like all of the intellectual and intuitive parts are turned fully on at the same time. This is when you are in your "zone" or "fulfilling your destiny" or "living your purpose". I have felt this way many times in the process of writing my speeches or delivering a speech to an audience, and also while learning about a fascinating new subject. Being creative can put you in your zone. An engineer who is designing a new product and loving the process easily gets lost in time. Getting that new invention out on the market can create a deep sense of satisfaction as well as pride. When we create products or services from this place of connection within ourselves, we give a gift to the world. What are the gifts that you'd like to share?

Being True to Yourself
Where to Draw the Line as the Boss?

Being in the boss role can be difficult when your boundaries are challenged by conflicts with others or issues concerning your business. Finding solutions for resolving conflicts and making compromises that you can feel good about isn't always easy. Every day we make choices, some turn out better than others.

We must live with the consequences from every decision we make. We learn from these experiences. Our choices may not be "right" or "wrong," just the best course of action in response to resolving a particular issue or situation.

One business owner had an employee who was impossible to work with due to their huge personality conflicts. It would have been best for both parties and the business for this employee to be laid off and sent on his way with a letter of recommendation and compensation. Instead, due to the details of this contract and the business laws in Canada, the boss could not lay off this employee without possible legal consequences. Resolution was difficult to find under these circumstances. The compromise this owner made was to attempt to "get along" with the challenging employee. Finally, after five years of struggling in their relationship, the employee found another job and moved on. In hindsight, was it worth the stress and anxiety to tolerate the situation that long? Would it have been better for the owner to suffer some financial losses in exchange for more peace of mind at work? Knowing where to draw the line and when becomes more apparent with experience. Sharing your experiences with other entrepreneurs can help you and others to prevent making poor choices with undesirable and even devastating consequences.

The Boss with No Boundaries

Here is an extreme case of boundaries not being set, to the point of destroying business relationships, and the business itself.

An entrepreneur, who we will refer to as "the boss", was growing his company at a very impressive rate. He was overwhelmed and needed to hire a general manager, who we will refer to as the "gm" which he did.

The gm stepped in spouting high praises of himself and boasted of the great things he would do for the company (first red flag: people who are good at what they do, do not have to say it out loud. It's evident). As the boss proceeded to use his talents in other parts of the company and let the gm do the business of running it, complaints started rolling in. Employees complained about rude verbal abuse they were getting from the gm. The staff complained that they were asked to do more than what was expected for their job, and were not allowed to leave until a task was done. Eight employees left their job because of the abusive manager. These were eight really good employees that the boss had a great relationship with. The employees who stayed on struggled to understand how the boss could tolerate such extreme behaviour from the gm.

Then there were the complaints from the suppliers and customers. Because of the gm's abrasive and rude conduct one major customer terminated doing business with the boss and his company. Suppliers were not willing to cooperate with the company anymore either. Customers and suppliers were drawing a line. All the years of groomed relationships that the boss had fostered were disappearing and in anger. The company's reputation was destroyed.

The boss would gently tell the gm that this behaviour was not acceptable. The gm would respond by yelling, using extremely foul language, or throwing a temper tantrum. The boss would crawl away hoping the gm would be in a better mood the next day. Then there were the emails from the gm to the boss, using profanity and advising him what he could and could not do. For example, the boss took a day off and the gm told him to get back to work and he had no right to be spending time away from the office. This message was laced with demeaning verbal abuse and many 'f' words. The boss ignored the message. No boundaries were ever laid.

While this was going on, the gm was persuading employees behind the boss's back to come with him to the new company he was creating. The gm wanted to get rid of the boss and own the company. His plan was to drive the present company into the ground, and buy it from the boss at a cheap price. Then he'd rebuild and grow it into a big success.

The gm had intentionally mismanaged the finances of the company to the point where the boss was forced to prepare for bankruptcy. Finally, the boss got legal advice and got rid of the general manager. An accountant was brought in to study the books and evidence of illegal money management put the gm in a position of being sued (which the boss never did). After the gm was fired, he had his lawyer send a threatening letter stating his intention to sue the boss (which he never did because of the risk of exposing his illegal financial management).

The cost of having this company drained to nothing was one million dollars.

What can we learn from this lesson?

Mistake #1: The boss was not looking over the gm's shoulder to make sure he was doing his job as expected ("The resume was so impressive").

Mistake #2: The boss was not drawing a line and setting a boundary the first time the gm's behavior was out of line, or the second time, or the third time ...

Mistake #3: The boss believed that if he ignored the gm long enough, things would change and get better.

Mistake #4: The boss avoided conflict at the cost of his dignity, self-esteem, and eventually the business. You might say that the boss did not have much dignity and self-esteem to begin with or this never would have happened. I say the boss needed to set his own clear boundaries and stand up for them.

Mistake #5: The boss needed to make a more thorough background check. When hiring employees, owners need to dig deep enough to find out about mental disorders. What medications are being used? Yet, legally we are not entitled to know all that is necessary. There are other ways to find clues. Have long detailed conversations with past employers. Not only take out both the husband and wife for dinner, but also have a few more meet and greets. Try something that is longer than a couple of hours and is tiring so you can see how one reacts under those conditions. Have planned conflicts come up during the day outings. If you are going to trust your business with someone, take the time to really get to know that person as much as possible. People do become masters at covering up their issues yet under stress or conflict there may be some little clues.

What examples of not setting boundaries in your life can you recall that cost you an expensive lesson either financially or emotionally? Did you learn from your lessons or will you be repeating them?

A Boss With Boundaries

Be warned: getting results from the boundaries you set may take some time. This boss in the following story, unlike the boss in the previous story, did have strong boundaries. Yet the time, energy and cost, both financially and emotionally, of dealing with incapable and unruly employees can be draining. This boss chose to act on the red flags every time they showed up.

The boss hired an employee (who we will call Bert) who had no respect for authority or boundaries in the workplace. Bert regularly disregarded the company policies and enjoyed the fight to justify his negative behaviour. He seemed to be one of those people who needed to be the centre of attention and negative attention was better than none. His constant overriding of the boss's authority was a regular issue. The boss knew that he would have to take legal action to fire this man, so he began the process of documenting every incident. Here are examples of these incidents.

The company policy of having projects approved required an in-person interview along with a formal written submission. Bert phoned a fellow employee at home, demanding that the employee's project proposal be given verbally over the phone, right then and there. The intimidated employee complied. The boss got the written proposal, but it did not sound like the work of the employee whose name was written at the bottom. Bert had written up the proposal and changed it to meet his needs and forged the employee's signature at the bottom of the page. When Bert was confronted with this situation, he completely denied it. The other employee filed a complaint of bullying.

Bert's compulsive behaviour also became problematic. He would obsess over a point and insist that he was right in spite of the fact that he didn't know what he was talking about. He called people names and would regularly insult them. Everyone thought that tactfulness and thoughtfulness were beyond him but he knew how to use them as a façade when necessary.

The situation cost several people seven months of stress and emotional energy that interfered with the productivity of the business. It took a formal, legal procedure, but eventually Bert was dismissed. Bert had no idea of how to set boundaries for himself or how to respect the boundaries of his fellow employees. The owner took it upon herself to make sure the employees and business were not going to be undermined by such an individual. She drew strong lines and would not allow them to be eroded. Again, sometimes to protect these boundaries, it is draining and time consuming when we have better things to pursue for the sake of business. Yet, action must be taken so the business can be successful.

To protect yourself from having problematic situations going on longer than necessary, consider the following questions:
- When have you known you needed to take a stand and be proactive yet did not? Was it because you were too busy or

too tired or wanted to avoid conflict?

- What were the consequences of not taking immediate action? How much did it cost you? Did it cost you money? An employee? A relationship?
- What would you do differently next time?

Drawing Clear Boundaries

How does an entrepreneur live with issues at work that go against what they believe to be right? Education and experience will teach them to avoid these kinds of mistakes in the first place. But when a problem does come up (and it will), brainstorm all possibilities, get professional help if necessary, and learn to cut your losses. The goal is to deal with the situation as quickly as possible and lower the stress levels of everyone involved. This is where "fierce conversations" need to happen, as suggested by Susan Scott (author of *Fierce Conversations*). The founder of Fierce, Inc., Scott has worked with many executives, including those from Fortune 500 companies, to improve communication and promote more honesty in the corporate environment. Scott offers ways for you to communicate with respect and integrity yet to the point. Her forthright advice on communication and problem solving is helpful for business as well as for your personal life. I believe in finding solutions, yet also recognize that some solutions may not yield a best-case scenario. A course of action that moves people forward, one way or another, is better than living with stress and anxiety in the workplace.

Friends and Partners: Can It Work?

If you have sacrificed your true self in a relationship with an employee because you were trying to be "nice" and a friend, chances are it turned out badly. Like parenting, the boss cannot be a friend. Generally speaking, parents have to choose between being a parent or being a friend to their children. The boss needs to make the same decision. Children lose respect for parents who are their friend first. Employees will lose respect for the boss when strong business leadership is compromised. Clear boundaries between the business and the personal, always make doing business easier and more efficient.

If you decide to go into business with a friend, sooner or later you will have to make a decision that forces you to draw the line between business and friendship. Conflicts that result because of differences in values, beliefs, and personalities will strain any business relationship. The problem is that some of those issues do not become apparent until well into the business relationship. If you haven't drawn up a written contract, you absolutely should. Unforeseen events will happen and there needs to be legal strategies for handling potential differences. Always have a "shot gun" clause. This provides both parties with the knowledge of what will happen when there is no resolution to a conflict and it gives you a way to dissolve the business relationship.

When friendships develop through being in business together, being upfront about the lines of business and lines of friendship are necessary. For example, if you have your business issues and agreements in writing, then neither party should expect those boundaries to waiver in business. If the lines become hazy, then one or the other person may begin to feel taken advantage of. The giving and taking in the business relationship should be agreed upon and honoured. (Actually, the same is true for a personal relationship. Any relationship will eventually crumble when one person is contributing more than the other and feeling used.)

A business relationship should never have to be compromised because of a friendship. Yet I have seen this happen all too often. If you have friends that you do business with, what takes priority for you, the friendship or the business relationship? If you had to choose between one or the other, which one would win?

I am not suggesting that mixing business with friendships is impossible. I am saying that when you do it, do it with clear boundaries and beware of the conflict of interests. Have a plan to handle the conflicts. Be firm in the lines that you draw around the business aspect of the relationship.

Wearing Different Hats

I have a business associate who is a close friend as well. We started out doing business together and had a written contract signed and money exchanged. A very precious friendship has developed while doing business. In an attempt not to have our business boundaries disrespected, I have made my request for strong lines between the two realms. I will say when changing course in conversation from business to friendship, "I am taking off my business hat now and putting on my friendship hat." Sometimes in a friendship conversation I will do the same. This metaphor of "hats" and being clear about which one I am wearing for which conversation, I find very helpful. I do not want my friend ever to feel taken advantage of in business with me or vice versa. Our business relationship must not be compromised. The boundaries must be respected for both of us. I feel this protects our friendship, our business, and our integrity. I also want all our agreements and expectations to be in writing so we both know where we stand and there is no ambiguity. A dual relationship like this does require the ability to be forthright. To be forthright requires vulnerability. To be vulnerable requires self-awareness and trust. All of these require the ability to set boundaries for yourself and respect others' boundaries as well.

When it comes to money, no special deals are made for friends. If my fee is $150, then I expect my friend to pay that amount. If my friend is not paying that amount, then I could be with a client who would be. This is my boundary. Business is business, money is money, and friends are friends. No muddy lines. I do not expect any discounts, deals, promotions or fringe benefits because of our friendship. The exchange of money and or services must be fair and equal to both parties.

Life may present situations where one would want to be flexible and "bend the rules". This is fine as long as being "flexible" does not mean that your boundary is completely stomped on. Be clear on your limits. Only you will know what is appropriate for you.

The "exchange of energy" must be equal. If it is not, one person will give more than the other and the imbalance will cause resentment. The resentment will kill the relationship both in the business and in the friendship.

Sex in the Workplace - Say No? or Go with the Flow?

Consider the boundaries that you feel are appropriate in your relationships with employees to avoid sex scandals at work. There can be many negative consequences for those who decide to go down the road to greater familiarity. An example would be when the boss is having an affair with an employee and one person wants to end it. The boss and this employee will still have to work together. If the boss lays their lover off work, then the boss runs the risk of angry legal repercussions. If the employee ends the affair, a rejected and spiteful boss may make it difficult for this person to work in the company. If they both agree to end the affair, the possible awkwardness may make it difficult to work in the same place.

Many men and women have had affairs with fellow workers and have stories to tell of how badly the affair ended. Movies are made based on the anger of the betrayed spouse or the scorn of a rejected lover in an affair. Maybe you remember the movie "Fatal Attraction". Or the real- life story of a wife who found out about her husband's affair and advertised it on a billboard. The scandal ruined her husband's career. Look at all the politicians and celebrities who deal with the fallout from affairs in the media.

Mixing business with pleasure, sooner or later, can get messy. Is it worth it? Do you care? Where do you set your boundaries? Have you, as a business owner, thought about these issues and decided how to handle them in your work environment?

The Power of the Pay Cheque

The power behind the money and the conflicts that can surface between employer and employee because of it go far beyond the issues of sex in the workplace. It is difficult for any CEO to hire people who are in exact alignment with the mission statement of the company and the values of the individuals involved. The hot issues that develop between people can be endless and this is where management can be challenging. Religion, politics, and sex are the most obvious areas that can cause potential conflict.

The Work Ethic

We're all familiar with the ruthless drive and dedication of successful entrepreneurs and the exhausting jet-set lifestyle that goes with it. The trend in the twenty-first century to care more about our health is redefining what success means in business. Success is no longer just about the money. More and more entrepreneurs are aiming for balance in their lives regarding work, relationships, health, and playtime. The work ethic is evolving. This is not to imply that hard work and long hours are not necessary and embraced by those who love what they do for a business. But the extreme of allowing ourselves to work excessively at the expense of our health and relationships is no longer a lifestyle that is considered acceptable. We need clear boundaries that embrace and enhance both our personal goals as well as our business goals.

Time Management

The difficulty of finding a balance between work time and personal time is an issue for most employees. Many struggle with pursuing their career goals while also finding time for partners and children. Focused entrepreneurs and CEOs look at the bottom line and are pressured to meet the financial goals. Their focus is not on how happily married the staff is. The state of their employees' personal lives rarely even crosses their minds. A strong work ethic and running a successful company is the number one priority. The high-tech industry is famous for expecting long hours per week from its workers. Those who are not willing to work 60-80-hour weeks end up with no job. The employee knows there are people to replace those who set boundaries and stand up to demand balance in their lives.

Although it will be a while yet before dramatic change takes place in the corporate world, these companies are being challenged. People are getting burned out with the "all work and no play" lifestyle that these kinds of jobs demand. They're looking for a better balance and settling for less pay. We also see a rise in new entrepreneurs coming into the corporate world who set more realistic boundaries for their employees in regards to work schedules. Increasingly, the entrepreneurs themselves want more vacation time and a reasonable work schedule. But there are still plenty of old school CEOs who look down their nose at those who set a boundary in their business life and demand balance. I would like to ask those of you who fit into this category to consider the impact of working those long hours: How is your health? Your stress level? Are you happy in your relationships?

What are your expectations for yourself and your employees when it comes to hours of work needed to get the job done? If one of your employees says "No" and sets a limit on doing any additional work, or staying late at work (maybe due to time constraints and or work overload, deadlines, etc.) would you fire this employee? Would you be open to discussing the situation to make things work for both of you? Do your employees comply with the hours because they need the job and you sign the pay cheque? Do they love what they do and enjoy working long hours? Have you had any "fierce conversations" with your employees on this subject?

Leadership Is Earned Not Given

We all can think of someone from our past or present experience that we would classify as a great leader!

What are the qualities that define a great leader? Much is written about this topic and there are many different points of view. In *Derailed*, author Tim Irwin discusses the positive and negative characteristics of a leader. Irwin states that in deciding between character and competence, character wins out in importance for a successful business leader. The qualities with the greatest impact are courage, authenticity, wisdom, and humility. On the negative side of leadership qualities, Irwin lists arrogance, self-promotion, inability to listen to others, lack of self-awareness, and lack of personal growth. When you see someone with arrogance, it's also apparent that self-awareness is lacking. The two do not go hand in hand.

My Top Picks for Positive Leadership Characteristics

1. The leader with integrity. I cannot think of one respected leader who did not have integrity. I can think of many examples of leaders who fell in the eyes of their followers when they were exposed as liars or hypocrites. We see a lot of examples in politics. I also see it many times in CEOs and the leaders of companies, large and small. A common example of this is the leader who claims to value honesty yet is lying to his wife since he is having an affair with the secretary. There is a huge disconnect between the words and the behaviour. What I look for in a leader, my friends, and myself is a clear connection between the verbal claims of who we are and the behaviour. So what do we do about the integrity issue with our leaders? Where do we draw the line of what we will or will not accept? I believe this is an individual choice with an individual boundary. We cannot make a hard and fast rule because of this hazy line between individuals. My degree of flexibility may be very different than yours. We all can at least

agree that integrity needs to be a foundational value for great leadership.

2. The leader who helps an individual yet leaves that person's dignity intact.

3. The leader with a plan A, plan B, and plan C. A committed leader has plans and fall back plans to ensure success. This starts with the business plan, mission statement, company policies, and a manifesto. What is your exit strategy? Even if you feel you will be working in this company indefinitely, an exit strategy is a must. We cannot predict what the future will bring so we need to cover all our bases. Always have a plan A, a plan B and a plan C.

4. The leader who leads by example. Actions do speak louder than words. People have high expectations of those in leadership roles. If you are not "walking the talk", your credibility is gone. Respect from others will be impossible.

5. The leader with humility. Tim Irwin explains in his book *Derailed*, that humility is difficult in our competitive business culture yet is vital to any long-term successful company. Humility is the ability to recognize the weaknesses and strengths of yourself and others all the while being respectful.

6. The leader who is a lifelong learner. Learning should include the intellectual, social, and emotional growth. Be open to personal development and greater self-awareness.

7. The leader with good communication skills. Keep everyone informed and when you do, chose your words wisely so your messages are clear. Mean what you say. Say what you mean. Avoid judgment.

8. The leader who is sensitive to others. Learn to appreciate the feelings, the needs, and the desires of other people. Avoid arrogance.

Teamwork Works!
Build Your Business with Strong Teams

Patrick Lencioni gives ideas on dealing with conflict and team building in *The Five Dysfunctions of a Team*. He recommends having team members that are trustworthy, open, honest, committed, accountable, and focused on the team results.

It can be difficult to find team members who are self-aware and mature enough for constructive feedback, able to admit their mistakes, and ask for help. Egos may get in the way of a successful team. Get to know your prospective players carefully. Have an experienced team leader who can foster growth and navigate through conflicts.

In order to communicate in meaningful ways, education on what is expected can go a long way. I would suggest bringing in qualified leaders to give seminars on ways to communicate in a team setting that honours and respects all the members.

Accountability of team members is vital to the success of the business. Without it, goals and plans fall apart and the company dwindles away to nothing. I believe that accountability starts with having everything in writing. This will keep all information available to refer back to. There will be no "he said," "she said". Make sure that all meetings are recorded and everyone has a chance to review the notes. Get written approval on the notes of the meeting from everyone so that there are no disagreements on the information.

Do you have examples in your corporate circles of great teams and not so great teams? What do you see as key elements for building your own team?

The Mission Statement - Companies with Purpose

Every business owner needs to begin with the mission statement. Without it, the company lacks direction and boundaries, leaving the door wide open for failure. On the flip side of this, look at the success of companies with clear mission statements. Strong mission statements draw strong boundaries and make implementing company policies much easier.

lululemon

This company has covered all its bases and has established a reputation for quality not only in its products but how the company is run on every level. The corporate governance, investor information, its manifesto, career opportunities and product services information, are all on its website flashing the values of quality and integrity.

Holy Crap Cereal

Corin and Brian Mullins started a company selling an all-natural cereal with low-calories, high nutrients, and great taste. It was on the shelves selling, but not quickly until they changed the name to Holy Crap and then the product flew off the shelves. They quickly had to be clear on their direction and be able to set boundaries and stay focused. Here is what the Mullins had to say: "We have a guiding principle ...We all know about the amazing health benefits of our cereal so we have a moral responsibility to distribute our cereal to as many people as possible. All of our growth is based upon that principle. In an explosive growth company it makes our decisions much easier to make."

The company owners have clarity with respect to their mission statement, or in their words, a "guiding principle".

Freshii

Matthew Corrin, founder of Freshii's Restaurant, wrote a five-point manifesto that is the basis for how he runs his business. Here are the five points from his interview on Inc.com:

1. Talk is cheap. Execution sets you apart.
2. Launch fast, fail fast, iterate faster.

3. Numbers rule.
4. Build a company with a killer culture not a culture that kills the company.
5. Pick your battles.

These basic yet fundamental rules in business are not new, but I like the way Corrin is short and precise. I agree that each one of these points is vital to any business that wants to succeed and expand.

When you create your mission statement or manifesto, consider how big you want your company to be. Are you happy with where it is now? Do you want to grow the company and by how much?

Take time to make the effort to really think through your mission statement. From that will stem your policies, work culture, and manifesto.

Professional Code of Ethics

Have you written a code of ethics for your business?

A professional code of ethics is a written set of guidelines that reflect the values and ethical standards of a company. These guidelines are designed to direct the actions of the employees and, of course, the employer. You will find how-to information and examples of codes of ethics at many online websites and in various books. My point is to bring this to your attention to put on your "to do" list if it is not already in place for your business.

Creating Your Work Culture

Entrepreneurs are setting new boundaries when they create new and positive work cultures. The flavour of the work culture varies from business to business. If you have not already created an outstanding work culture with your employees, think about doing so now. Happier employees translates into more profits in the end. What values do you want to start with? Integrity? Communication? Quality of work? Fun?

Here is an example of how I created a work culture centered on my values for health and wellness. As a consultant in the health and wellness industry, I strongly encourage a work culture that supports nutrition, fitness, and life balance.

The benefits:
- Healthier employees.
- Less employee absenteeism.
- Increased productivity from employees with more energy and health, which translates to better financial health for the company.
- A corporate reputation for a great place to work, which means easier recruitment.
- Employees are likely to stay with the company longer.
- Less internal health care costs.

Suggestions for boosting health awareness in your work place

Educate your employees with lunch-and-learn seminars or one to three hour training sessions on topics of nutrition, fitness, stress, sleep, mental health, brain health, or any other topic under the heading of wellness.

1. Have the vending machines filled with healthy snacks and water.
2. At meetings, offer healthy alternatives to the usual sweets, pastries, coffee and tea, such as, fruit and veggie platters, water and herbal teas.
3. Encourage employees to do a walk or run event under the corporate name.
4. Offer gym memberships as prizes or incentives.
5. Provide shower facilities for those wishing to run or cycle to work.
6. Offer a fitness challenge. Some people love a challenge on a fun basis.

7.   Set the example as the leader of your company.

All of the wellness habits for physical health spill over into enhancing one's brain health. Supporting everyone's health in the work environment contributes to the morale of the company. Being supported in a group goes a long way to encourage and inspire better attitudes and camaraderie.

Policies for Cell Phones in the Workplace

A respectable work culture should include some boundaries around cell phones. These policies need to be communicated to everyone in a written statement, and the policies for their use in the workplace need to be maintained. For example, the code of conduct for meetings could include a cell phone policy. Maybe employees could leave their phones in their offices and come to the meeting without them. Or maybe have everyone put their cell phones in box at the door and collect them on the way out at the end of the meeting. People reading messages, texting, and googling while in a meeting is not acceptable behaviour. It distracts from the business at hand. We need to establish cell phone etiquette and make it part of our social culture.

Designing a More Positive Work Culture

Take a look at the companies whose owners have designed positive work cultures that reflect a code of ethics appropriate for that business. lululemon, founded by Chip Wilson, designs and manufactures high-quality yoga clothing that can be worn for various purposes. The website uses the following words to describe their code of conduct: "quality, integrity, balance, fun, greatness, fairness, honesty" (www.lululemon.com).

The million-dollar-plus recycling company 1-800-GOT JUNK? founded by the visionary Brian Scudmore, is another company with a reputation for its exceptional work culture. This is a company that emphasizes strong communication in the workplace. Employees are encouraged to share their mistakes as lessons on how to improve the business.

What are your company's ethics? How do they enhance your workplace?

Setting Boundaries for Successful Business Relationships

These are six simple, yet not always followed, rules for protocol in business. They will set the stage for smooth interactions in the workplace.

Rule #1: Always put business agreements in writing! It is much easier to point to the mission statement, manifesto, code of conduct, code of ethics, job description, financial budget, minutes of the meeting, and decisions made, if they are in writing. Have the appropriate documents to support your agreements. Whenever any kind of meeting is held, follow up the verbal communications with a written account of what was said and get the other parties approval on the written report.

Rule #2: Have witnesses to conversations and agreements when appropriate.

Rule #3: Do not embarrass or humiliate others or use sarcasm as a form of communication.

Rule #4: Do not be a control freak. Always give people choices.

Rule #5: Be kind and respectful.

Rule #6: Be short and to the point. Be concise but not so short that needed explanations are left out. You may be in a situation where justification is warranted. Avoid long meandering conversation. Avoid long justifications that are not necessary.

The Executive's Health and Wellness Plan

The leader of the company is encouraged to set the example for healthy living habits in their workplace. But the need for the boss to embrace these habits goes far beyond setting an example. I can share many stories of entrepreneurs who struggle with health issues around stress, lack of nutrition, exercise and lack of life balance. Yet these stories are not uncommon. Typically, being driven to succeed, translates into long hours, wearing many hats, and dealing with various stressful issues. Nobody ultimately cares about the success of the business more than the owner. Nobody has as much at risk, financially and emotionally, as the owner. The challenge to take care of one's own health can be overwhelming most of the time. The consequences of continually abusing your body through poor nutrition, lack of exercise, lack of regular sleeping habits, and excess stress will bring you to your knees sooner or later, in one way or another.

Exercise - It's Not a Luxury!

If you live and breathe your work from morning until bedtime, there is little time for exercise. Let's face it, those of us who make time for exercise know it's a commitment and time consuming. When the problems at work are in absolute need of your attention, it is difficult to walk away for an hour plus to work out. By the end of the day, fatigue takes over and there is no energy left to exercise. Many business owners are overweight and seriously out of shape because of this issue. Busy people need to make a plan to work out and commit. There needs to be a plan A and a plan B for when the regular schedule gets neglected due to some necessity.

The consequences of a lifetime without regular exercise can be devastating. To mention a few: heart attacks, poor brain health, Type 2 diabetes, breast cancer, colon cancer, and obesity. Other issues that can result from no exercise include: high blood pressure, high blood sugar, high cholesterol, digestion problems, lower testosterone, sleep problems, stiff joints, unhealthy bones (bones need weight-bearing exercise), depression, decreased cognitive function, mood swings, and imbalanced hormone levels. Decreased blood flow and oxygen affects not only your brain but your sexual performance as well. This fact alone should motivate most of you (men) to get up from your desks and run to the gym before finishing this paragraph. Did I mention that exercise increases your energy level too?

Eating for Life - Nutrition Made Easy

The classic problem with getting enough nutritious food when working long hours is due to not planning for snacks and meals. Eating on the run usually means skipping meals or eating restaurant food that is high in fat, salt, sugar, and calories. Keeping energy levels up with caffeinated beverages, energy drinks, and the long list of junk foods is deadly to one's health. It should be no surprise that you feel completely drained and spent by the end of the day.

Pre-planning need not be complicated. Think protein, healthy carbohydrates, and healthy fats (see Chapter 5 on health for guidance). To get started, visit the grocery store to find quick snacks to sustain you. Suggestions:

- Protein: Have some hard-boiled eggs or chicken or fish leftovers in the fridge at work.
- Healthy Fats: Think omega 3. A trail mix with raw nuts and seeds is an easy choice. Avocados are great plain or with a little salt and pepper, maybe lemon juice if you like it.
- Healthy Carbohydrates: There are many fruits and vegetables to choose from that can be washed quickly at the office. Or better yet, buy a ready-to-eat tray. No prep required.
- Keep a stash of the above nutrients in your office and in your car.

These tips may sound obvious and elementary, but unless you make a conscious effort to become more aware of your diet and get disciplined about it, chances are you won't change. Great plans are useless without execution.

Prioritize Sleep

I don't need to tell you how much sleep you need to be getting at night. Your body is already communicating that to you loud and clear. You will not be able to hear your body's message if you have pumped it up with drugs and caffeine or if you are suffering from anxiety and insomnia. Some people need more sleep than others. Whatever your ideal number of hours for sleep is, make sure to get it. Lack of sleep inevitably affects your ability to function intellectually and emotionally (see Chapter 5 on health for more details on sleep facts).

It's extremely difficult to be your best when you cannot concentrate or remember what someone said ten minutes ago. Where is sleep on your list of priorities?

Stress - The Good, the Bad, and the Deadly!

We all have stress at one time or another in our lives. It's inevitable. Stress can be a good thing in balanced doses. On the positive side, the adrenaline produced by stress makes us more focused, alert, and gives us more energy to slay our dragons. We are stimulated into fight or flight responses very quickly. On the down side, too much stress for extended periods of time; for example, months and or years can be a disaster to your mental and physical health. This can lead to major relationship issues both at home and at work that can end up beyond repair. The following story illustrates that possible scenario.

"The Life of an Entrepreneur"

It was five thirty in the morning and the entrepreneur was having a shower before running off to the office. Everyone in the house was awake because they could hear all the extremely loud, cussing and swearing from the shower. This was not an unusual morning. The stresses at work were causing such anxiety and anger that sooner or later the boss's health would suffer. And so it did. A couple of years later, he was flat on his back at home for two months while he waited for surgery. Stress can manifest its effects in many kinds of illnesses or disease. It could be cancer or heart disease.

Entrepreneurs are usually out of balance because of their high-stress lifestyles. First, they have all the issues of the business stressing them out. With only 24 hours in a day and so much to do, the stress from lack of sleep, improper nutrition, and lack of exercise adds up quickly. Basic human requirements for health are not being met. The mind and body can only take so much abuse before something breaks down. So what are you willing to let go of? You cannot do it all. Are you going to delegate more? Are you going to adjust your expectations for your business goals? Are you going to acknowledge to your family that you can't do it all? Are you willing to give up time with your children? Are you willing to give up your marriage? Where will you draw the line?

Our culture in North America has taught us that we can be wonderful companions and exceptional parents at the same time as pursuing passionate, all engulfing careers. The concept of spending "quality" time with our loved ones has almost been degraded into a rationalization for spending less time with them to meet the demands of our work goals. When we get to the point where our family or our business is struggling because we have spread ourselves too thin, we feel inadequate. We have been misled into thinking we can do it all. The truth is: we cannot.

These unrealistic expectations will drive you to feeling inadequate, a failure, and depressed. Something or someone is going to suffer. How will your business do if you're in the hospital? How happy will your wife and children be if they never see you or share a meal with you all week, week after week, for years? If you decide to live a life of non-stop stress and continually ignore your health and or relationships, then something in your life is bound to change. Your body may say "No" to being abused and succumb to cancer. A relationship that has been neglected could deteriorate to the point that your partner decides to leave you. Wouldn't it be better for you to make the decision to take care of your health, your relationships, and your business? This is a place in your life where serious boundaries need to be set. Either you can decide to be empowered by taking control of your life or to be a victim of what life decides will be your consequences for your lack of making your own decisions. What boundaries are you going to establish? Where are your deepest loves, passions, needs, and wants?

Do your priorities reflect that? Clear priorities lead to clear boundaries and in turn, less stress.

Your Love Life - Sex on the Run?

If you're a CEO or business owner, chances are you fit the profile of an overly stressed, career-driven individual who is lacking exercise, nutrition, and sleep. How is your love life? Is a healthy sex life a priority for you? How does your partner feel about this? If you are not taking care of your sexual needs at home, are the offerings at work looking very tempting? Is this what you really want? What is your partner doing about the lack of sex with you? Is there someone at home who is looking forward to spending some time in bed with you? What boundaries do you have to protect and honour a great sex life at home? Don't have one? Interested in making one? Just be honest here! Maybe sex is not a priority?

What Are Your Priorities?
Is Your Significant Other on the List?

An entrepreneur was asked to list his priorities in life in order of their importance. His wife thought that she would be in the top five of his list. When he shared his list of about 10-12 things, she was devastated. She wasn't on his list at all. When this was pointed out to him, she naively thought he would consider the point and put her somewhere on his list. Instead he justified it by explaining why all those things were so important to him, saying that he only had so much energy and time. The wife never made the list at all. That marriage eventually ended with the wife feeling unloved and uncherished. Most wives probably understand that there are times when the entrepreneur cannot put his partner on the priority list for a time. That is the compromise, but years and years of never being on that list is heartbreaking. The husband had made a conscious decision that his marriage would take the fall. This reflected his true priorities.

So I ask you entrepreneurs to make a plan for your life that reflects your deepest desires and loves. If your partner is not on that list, it is better to deal with it now than waste any more of your precious years or your partner's years. Usually fixing a relationship is possible when there is a willingness to do so on both sides. This would be my first choice. Is it yours? Or is it better to end it now? When do you decide to cut your losses?

I believe that every business owner needs to embark on many conversations with their partner about the lifestyle, goals, and sacrifices needed to make the business a success. The outcome of these conversations should end with a joint venture agreement (see details for this agreement at the end of the chapter). You need to be on the same team, not opposing teams.

Global Lines - Making a Difference

Once you have established yourself as a high-level leader and created a successful bridge between your relationships at home and your career, it is time to reach out and expand into the greater community, whether locally or globally.

In today's business environment it's good marketing strategy to attach your business to a "cause" that benefits something greater than just you and or your company. An example of this is 1-800-GOT JUNK? This recycling company has a proactive policy of not contributing to our landfills. Another example is Cobs,. this company makes fresh bread every day and actively supports environmentally conscious practices with a "green" artisan oven to reduce energy resources. Cobs has donated over ten million dollars in bread to different charities.

These companies combine good marketing strategies with a sincere mission to make a difference. When a business makes a superficial effort to "make a difference" for marketing reasons alone, the authenticity is lost. We as consumers want more. We recognize the marketing strategy behind the "do good" action and that's appropriate when the action is genuinely worthwhile.

Doing the Work!

Knowing When to Say "No!" or "Yes!"

If your intuition and or your head does not make it clear to you whether to set a boundary or not, consider the following questions.

1. Does the answer reflect staying on course with the mission statement and the policies?
2. Is there respect for yourself and the other person regarding the course of action?
3. Are you legally within the boundaries of the law?
4. Are you emotionally attached to an outcome regardless of whether or not it's the right thing to do?
5. Are you trying to be "nice" and allowing your business boundaries to be eroded?

Giving Your Gifts to the World

We all have our talents and gifts that we can make use of in our businesses. Are you cognizant of what your pluses are? Are you using them as fully as possible?

1. What are your gifts? Do you use them in business?
2. What is the outcome of your working in your "zone"? What do you produce or provide?
3. Does your mission statement reflect the real reason you are in business?
4. Does this reason reflect your true talents and passions?
5. Are you being authentic in your day-to-day conduct? If you are, your talents and gifts are being used to enhance your business.

Getting Your Company on the Path to Success

Here are some questions designed to help you clarify what you and your business are about. If you have not created a formal business plan, do so to establish goals and boundaries.

1. Review or write your mission statement.
2. What are your values and beliefs about how your company should be run?
3. Write or review the policies.
4. What are the consequences when the boundaries are not honoured in your company? Do you follow through?
5. As a leader, do you mean what you say and say what you mean? Do your actions back up your words?
6. List your present leadership qualities, both positive and negative.
7. Do your leadership skills need improving? Be honest. What resources would help you improve?
8. Are you financially responsible with the company's money? Have you a knowledgeable accountant and lawyer to guide you in sound practices?
9. Is there balance in terms of time spent at work and downtime?

For you? For the employees? What are the vacation terms in the company's policies?

Know Your Priorities
Setting the Boundaries for Success

Without being clear on your priorities, your time and energy could end up being wasted on things that have little or no value to you. This is vital to setting boundaries around everything in your life.

1. List your priorities - all of them, including your personal needs.
2. Where are the basics of health on this list? Sleep, nutrition, exercise, sex?
3. Where are your deepest loves, passions, needs, and desires? Do your priorities reflect this?
4. Which priorities are you willing to sacrifice or compromise on to be successful in your business?
5. There are only so many hours in a day. You only have so much energy before you are done. How can you do less and still have everything accomplished? Are you going to delegate more? Are you going to adjust your expectations of your business goals? Of yourself? Which ones?
6. Are you willing to give up time with your kids? Are you willing to give up your marriage?
7. Do you want to stay in this stressful state or change it? What actions are you taking to change your stress?
8. How well will your business do with you in the hospital? This is not sarcasm. Seriously make a plan for your unexpected absence. Who will cover for you? How much will this cost the company?
9. Which will cost you the most: a vacation or damage to your health that prevents you from working? Which will cost you the most, dinner at home once in a while, a vacation, or a

divorce? I am suggesting you seriously take a look at these numbers. A divorce is not cheap.

10. How is your sex life? Is it a priority for you? For your partner? Do you need to have a conversation with your partner?

Joint Venture Agreement with Your Significant Other

1. If you are in a relationship, design a joint venture agreement. Make sure your partner is a team player.

2. Each person should have a list of their priorities.

3. Go through the lists together to come up with a combined priority list that will be the basis for your joint venture agreement. You each will still have an individual priority list that is unique to you. For example, one of my priorities is to have time for my fitness goals such as cross country skiing. My partner might not have this in common with me. Hopefully we would have a shared priority of time for work (hours per day and week) and another one for relationship time (hours per day, week, month, vacations together).

4. Your agreement should list your financial plan and goals for your personal life and your business. Both parties need to be educated on the finances of the company in order to have a clear picture of why and how your lives will be impacted. Both of you need to agree on this plan to avoid the risk of potential conflict or resentment due to a lack of understanding and commitment.

Global Lines - Reaching Out to Help Others!

Find the cause that calls to you.

1. What can your business do to contribute to a worthy cause? Make it real! Make it significant! Make it count! Find a purpose where you are no longer willing to look the other way and do nothing. Draw a line of intolerance.

2. If your company or you personally are making financial contributions, do your due-diligence and find out where the money is actually going.

Conclusion

Bring All You Are to the Business
All Your Head and All Your Heart!

Bringing your best self to the business requires clarity on who you are, your code of ethics with your mental and physical health intact, knowing what your gifts (talents and passions) are and using them in the best way possible. To bring your best and thrive, your significant other needs to be on your team. Balancing all the needs and wants of yourself and all the team members (at home and at the office) requires honest and open communication and planning. Strong boundaries that are drawn with respect for all involved will empower everyone. Knowing when and where to be flexible with those boundaries allows for relationships to mature while still honouring core values. Compromising is necessary in business relations, but there is a fine line between too much and not enough. Practice setting your boundaries in order to fine tune them and learn where to draw the line.

Stand tall and strong with integrity and honour.

Chapter 7
Boundaries in the Workplace - Career Challenges, Career Choices

Coming together is a beginning; keeping together is progress;
working together is success.
Henry Ford

You may dream of enjoying some of your boss's luxuries, but you don't have to suffer through your boss's nightmares. That's the biggest advantage of being the employee of a business rather that the owner of one. Even though the employee takes the risk of getting laid off in bad times, the owner stands to lose everything invested in the business, not to mention being put out of a job. Most business owners wear many hats to keep things running smoothly, and often lie awake at night worrying about everything from finances to management issues. The responsibilities of an employee are far less demanding. Many employees can just shut the door, turn out the lights, and head home for the day. As an employee, it's best to weigh the pros and cons of your position so you can see things in perspective and feel happier with your job. If you are feeling dissatisfied, maybe it's because you feel taken for granted or your boundaries are being eroded away by someone or by something happening beyond your control in the workplace.

In this chapter, we will take a look at some of the reasons that employees have boundary issues in their workplace environments, and we'll consider ways that can empower you to be happier and more successful in your job and career.

Company Values versus Employee Values?

The best run company can have well-thought-out policies to promote the job satisfaction of its employees and still experience conflicts with some of the employees. This is far more likely to happen when an employee does not share the company values.

To give you a better chance of having a positive work experience as an employee, do some homework before you start a prospective job. Don't email your resume to apply for a job or set foot in a new workplace until you do some research into the company's mission and policies.

Do you support the company's mission and values?

Are you comfortable with the company's stated policies, rules etc.? Or would working in that environment mean compromising important boundaries?

Democracy or Dictatorship?

If you are an individual who views the workers of a company as a "team," and believes that a business should be run like a democracy where everyone has a say, then you would be very unhappy with an employer who feels that a successful business must be run like a dictatorship. In that scenario, the employee has no opportunity for participating in the running of the company and the decisions made. The employee is expected to abide by whatever the employer wants. The owner may feel that an authoritative style is justifiable since they are the one taking the financial risks and has far more knowledge about the business than the employee. There may be a certain amount of team building encouraged in the workplace, but the "boss" always makes the final decisions.

What would you do if you owned your own company? Would you run it like a dictatorship or a democracy?

Power of the Pay Cheque - Sell Out or Bail Out?

Most employees are at the mercy of their employers when it comes to their pay cheques. This is where the lines of our personal boundaries, our core values and beliefs, can be eroded. The pressure on the employee to perform at a certain level to keep up with company standards, just to keep getting that pay cheque, can be extreme. The high-tech industry in Silicon Valley is a classic example. For decades, the expectations of corporate management for employees to work long hours with tireless dedication has seriously jeopardized the employee's personal relationships, family life, and health. I don't think that many of those dedicated employees enjoy working stressful 80 hour weeks, forcing them to shortchange exercise, sleep, and time with friends and family. Yet, they keep on doing it because the pay is good, and they know that there are other well-qualified employees who would be more than willing to make these sacrifices to make the big bucks.

This is an example of how employee boundaries can be completely ignored by the "boss". That kind of corporate mentality puts the bottom line goal ahead of employee well being. The high-tech industry is a culture all its own.

Changing the Dream

Colin and Andrea met in Silicon Valley while working in the high tech industry. They got married, had three children, and both were employed at high paying jobs. After eleven years of the stress and sacrifice it takes to keep these careers, they decided to change their lifestyle. They moved to a rural area, bought a farm, and are now successful entrepreneurs. Colin and Andrea were wise enough to realize before buying the farm that running this business could be just as stressful as their previous careers. To make sure they did not end up feeling as stressed and unhappy as before, they came up with a plan to make their lives work differently. After eight years, Colin, Andrea and their children seem to have found their calling in life. Vacations, downtime, family time, and couple time are all part of the new life routine. It works for them. This is an example of how some people create the life they really want after allowing their boundaries to be virtually destroyed.

Taking the First Steps

Many people are not so lucky. Some feel they have no choice but to remain in stressful careers because it's all they know how to do. Most employees will not draw a line with the boss since it may cost them their job. In our competitive job market, speaking up may not seem worth the risk. The power of the one "who signs the pay cheque" rules. That doesn't mean you shouldn't begin to think about some options, and start dreaming about what you'd rather do for a living.

I suggest taking some time to be really clear on who you are and what you want (see Chapter 2 "Getting Clear"). Why compromise yourself? When you have that self-awareness, you will know what your life should look like to fulfill your need to be true to yourself. Then looking at your career and considering your whole situation with regards to family and financial responsibilities, you can decide a course of action.

The important thing is to take some action if you're feeling unhappy in your job. Start by taking steps that make sense to you. Maybe all you need to do is have a discussion with your boss about adjusting your hours. Maybe your boss can compromise on some of your requests and maybe you can meet half way. Maybe there's another career you would like to pursue. Without abruptly quitting your present job, you could start taking steps to transition into a new career. If education is needed, consider night courses or online courses so you can work at your own pace. Regardless of whether you think slow transition or a drastic change is what you need, doing something to work towards achieving happiness and fulfillment is what counts. Moving forward, even if that means just taking a few baby steps, is so much better for you than stagnating and feeling hopeless.

Getting Stuck - the Fear of Stepping Up

Bill was living pay cheque to pay cheque. His former boss had always paid him on the first and 15th of the month. On long weekends, Bill was paid on the Friday before the weekend even though the law states the owner wasn't required to pay him until after the weekend. So for twenty-five years, this was the policy Bill had become accustomed to. The new owner did not tell Bill that this arrangement was going to change. When the next long weekend came along, Bill anticipated receiving his cheque as usual, only to find out that he would not get paid until the following week. This would not sound like a big deal to many people, but to someone who lives from pay cheque to pay cheque, it was a problem. Bill desperately needed the money for rent and food. He felt unfairly treated, especially since some of the other employees did get paid that Friday. Why was he not paid the same day as the others? There was no explanation offered by the boss.

What were Bill's options? He could accept the change in policy and say nothing about it. Or, Bill could explain the situation to his new boss and ask for what he wanted. Bill needed to express his concerns and not allow his boundaries to be so blatantly stepped on. Yet Bill felt intimidated and said nothing, and now feels bitter and resentful towards his new boss. Every day Bill goes to work feeling stressed. Even if his boss hadn't given Bill what he wanted, if he had asked, at least he would have the satisfaction of knowing that he had stood up for himself and taken some responsibility. Bill does have the choice to not tolerate his unhappy situation. He could start looking for a new job while still working at the present one. Learning new tools for communicating will be a challenge for some. Most "bosses" will (or should) have conversations with employees about their concerns.

"Fierce Conversations"

Workplace situations where a lack of communication results in resentment and a stressful environment happen regularly. My number one suggestion for employees is to have "fierce conversations," as Susan Scott recommends in her book on workplace communication (*Fierce Conversations*). Fierce conversations are about being honest and upfront with other people, speaking your truth with respect while also listening to what others have to say. This is difficult to do when the parties involved are not educated and experienced in this type of communication. If you cannot have a respectful and direct conversation with your boss, then hire someone to be a mediator for you who understands Scott's method of communication. Everyone may think they know about open communication with respect and tactfulness but I find few do. If you are looking for a "business coach" or "life coach," be very careful that you find an experienced person, and get recommendations from previous clients. The first chapter on "experts" will help you with this. If speaking directly to your boss and or involving a mediator does not resolve the situation, then you need to consider your other options listed above. Planning an exit strategy may be the next step.

Sex in the Workplace

Workplace environments lend themselves to forming relationships with other people because you're on the job with each other so many hours each day. When tension builds up in the workplace or things get so routine that they're boring, some people find relief in having fantasies about their fellow colleagues or flirting with them. Where do you draw the line in your relationships with co-workers? Do you open the door to intimacy? Sexual relationships develop in the workplace all the time. The issue of boundaries is really up to the individual's values and beliefs. I don't believe that companies have much control over their employees' personal conduct decisions. The decisions we make around our sexuality are completely ours to make. Do I put my stamp of approval on having affairs with colleagues? For me, it would depend on whether someone is cheating on a spouse. That opinion is based on my core value. I am clear on my boundaries. Are you?

There may be a company policy discouraging sexual relationships between colleagues, but that doesn't necessarily stop anyone from controlling their lust. A great example of this is in the military. The rule is that men and women are not to have sexual relationships with each other, yet it happens regularly. How could it not when working and living in close quarters for long periods of time? Do you think we should change the rules and have more realistic boundaries? There is some common sense to this rule in the military. If two people are sexually and emotionally involved with each other while in combat, their ability to do a soldier's job may be compromised and lives are at risk. The same would apply in many work situations.

Sex and the Boss

It is a serious violation of personal boundaries when the boss solicits sexual favours from an employee in return for a salary or bonus. This practice has been going on for centuries. It's most common with male bosses and female employees, but it also occurs the other way around. In spite of the fact that a person can take legal action in our society, this does not solve the problem because it's so ingrained in society. Some employees (usually women) often need the job so badly that they're desperate to do anything to keep it – or to get the job in the first place.

If you are a woman in this situation, I would suggest seeking out not only the free legal service that is available but counselling as well. If you chose to sleep with the boss, do so with your eyes wide open and consider all the consequences first. This should be a choice you make, not a requirement for keeping the job. If your boss makes it a requirement, get out now. Seek legal help.

There should be no compromise on maintaining this personal boundary.

Are You Manipulating the Boss?

On the other side of the coin: Are you the one doing the manipulating? Women have been known historically to use their sexuality to get promotions and benefits from the boss because of their lower status in the work force. Sex sometimes works! Some male bosses are very aware of the game and happy to play it. Others are more naïve. When the boss is naïve, then the employee (female or male) who provides sexual favours in exchange for benefits is being manipulative. In that case, the boss needs to be self-aware and decide where to set the boundary. If you are the one doing the manipulating then you have set your boundary.

Money is Power
Compromising for Your Pay Cheque?

The fact that the boss is the one with the power may intimidate some employees. If you are easily intimidated, a journey of self-growth with personal counselling, workshops, or reading self-help books to find something that resonates with you would help to boost your self-esteem. Growing into a strong person who can set boundaries is empowering. This could help you avoid being in situations where you feel compromised or diminished.

Fair Pay Is Fair Play

Are you in a situation where your boss is eroding your time boundaries? Are you taken for granted? Are you paid fairly for the work that you do? Are you working for free? Why? Do you have a written contract with your employer that states the roles and responsibilities of the job (commonly known as the "job description") and the amount of pay in return? Do you keep track of your hours every day? You should. Both you and your boss need to know this kind of information. If you are expected to work a ten-hour day to accomplish your tasks and it is taking fourteen hours then both of you need to understand why. No working relationship or successful company can move forward without being clear on the operations of it. When the engine is not running smoothly as expected, it cannot be fixed unless you know where the problem is coming from. In this example, does the employer have unrealistic expectations of what a competent human being can do in ten hours? Or is the employee in need of more education or training in order to complete the tasks in the required time? Are you afraid to appear incompetent if you tell your boss you cannot complete requested tasks in the time frame asked for? Or maybe you do not know how to do the job to his/her satisfaction, in which case this needs to be shared so the boss can support you with more training. Are you made to feel inadequate because your workload is overwhelming? This is a huge red flag that your boundaries are being crossed.

Does your salary reflect your true worth based on actual time spent working? Try doing some research online. Look for your job and see what the average salary is for the same work experience you have. Is this in a comparable range to what you are being paid? Or do you find that you're being underpaid? If so, a conversation with your boss as to why this is the case may be extremely helpful. Before you can consider how to set fair boundaries, you need to get your facts in order and hear the boss' side of the story. There could be a list of explanations that make sense. Maybe the company is struggling financially and can't afford to pay employees what they're worth without going out of business. Then you have to ask yourself if you should be looking for a job elsewhere. Maybe the boss is unhappy with your work. In that case, find out what you need to do for the boss to feel you are worth a raise. This may entail picking up some courses to increase your professional development. Again, this situation needs investigation and some frank conversation with your employer. Then, and only then, can you set your boundaries with regards to the fairness of the salary you receive.

Electronic Communications in the Workplace

Our culture has been transformed by the advances in technology that give us computers, cell phones, iPads etc. These electronic gadgets and devices have become a way of life and no business could run without them. But these new technologies can be distracting and they interfere with good face-to-face communication and business relations in workplace environments. We need to make adjustments and set boundaries for a balanced use of these devices.

When you receive an email message from a business colleague or client that causes you to feel upset or emotional while responding, it's easy to write the message and press the "send" button and later regret it. I try to write and save my emotional emails as a draft first, and let the emotions settle for a while before sending. Note I said, "try". Sometimes the heat of the moment gets the best of me. Then there is the issue of how the reader will interpret our words in the email. Just like when you're composing a handwritten letter, take the time to choose your words carefully. It's easy to think that email correspondence doesn't matter that much because it's so quick and impermanent. But sending an email message that's negative or overly emotional can put you in a bad light and even cost you your job.

As much as it is a good idea to put everything in writing, it should not be at the expense of face-to-face conversation. Avoiding real-life conversations all the time can contribute to lack of communication via facial expressions, tone of voice and personal contact. Email is impersonal and keeps people at a distance. This is absolutely the best choice at times. At other times, it may be a problem. You will have to decide when email is appropriate for you and your colleagues and when a face-to-face conversation is best.

Work 24/7 - Cell Phone Slavery

The boundary between our personal time and our work time has been seriously eroded by the use of cell phones and computers. Back in the good old days before cell phones and computers, it was difficult for the boss to reach an employee at home, after work hours, or on time off. Now, no matter where an employee is, he or she can be interrupted by an email, text, or phone call from the boss. Where should the employee draw the line? Is it okay with you that your boss texts you in the middle of your family movie night with a request that needs to be done by tomorrow morning? Are you okay with having your vacation time interrupted by constant emails and texts requesting your immediate attention? Do you give yourself relief from work during mealtime or are you answering your text messages or phone calls then too? How about being interrupted with work messages during sex? Do you give in and ruin the mood to answer the requests? Wait! Why do your keep your cell phone in the bedroom? Wouldn't you prefer to have that space reserved for enjoying intimacy with your partner or a good night's sleep?

The pressure of always having to be "on the job" with no real downtime because of cell phones and computers has to contribute to our stress levels. The only way out of this constant "on" mode is to be responsible about setting our boundaries in order to turn the "off" switch. Our downtime preserves our sanity and lowers our stress level so we are more able to cope with the stress that builds up at work. So does your boss overstep the line with you in your personal life? What about your colleagues?

Electronic Devices at Meetings - the Invisible Employee

Every workplace environment should have protocol in place for the use of electronic devices during meetings. In my experience as a facilitator in meetings, I feel annoyed when members of the group choose to read or text on their laptops and or cells phones. My boundary as the person in charge is to request that cell phones be turned off and ignored during a meeting. I would like all those in the room to be fully present and part of the discussion. My flexibility on this issue comes into play when a person lets me know they will need to answer a call or text message that they are expecting and the timing of it is crucial and unavoidable. As a person who has sat in meetings and not been the one in charge, I still feel it is disrespectful to the group to be preoccupied with the cell phone.

A respectable work culture should include some boundaries around cell phones. These policies need to be communicated to everyone in a written statement, and the policies for their use in the workplace need to be enforced. For example, the code of conduct for meetings could include a cell phone policy. Maybe employees could leave their phones in their offices and come to the meeting without them. Or maybe set a policy for everyone to put their cell phones in a box at the door and collect them on the way out at the end of the meeting. People reading messages, texting, and googling while in a meeting is not acceptable behavior. It distracts from the business at hand. We need to establish cell phone etiquette and make it part of our work culture.

Here are some questions to help you think about setting your own boundaries:

Have you found a balance for using cell phones and electronic gadgets in your business life? Are your boundaries respectful of the situation?

What is your protocol for cell phones, texting, emailing, and iPads in the workplace?

Is there a conflict of boundaries with anyone at work when using these devices? At meetings?

Say "No" to Bullying in the Workplace

Bullying is an unacceptable violation of boundaries. It is hurtful and disrespectful. Some people will be unable or unwilling to respect other's boundaries. This is where you need to stand up for yourself. Some situations require getting outside help in order to set a strong boundary. If need be, legal action may be required. If the cost of getting legal help is an issue, Google "Free Legal Aid" and enter the name of your city to find legal support. Reach out for help in any case because saying, "No" to bullying is a must. If you see someone else being bullied, be open to helping that person reach out to find proper help. The more people who take a stand against those who bully others in the workplace, the stronger the message we send.

Boundary Exercises for Employees

You may be stewing about issues at work that cause you stress. You may feel intimidated by your boss. You may not know what is the best course of action in a particular situation. Think carefully and be honest with your answers when answering the following questions.

1. Are you being compromised in any way by your employer? If so, how? Do you compromise yourself because you need the job and the pay cheque? Would drawing a line and setting a boundary result in losing your job?
2. All relationships, whether in business or at home, require some flexibility to make them work. The question you want to be clear about is to what extent are you willing to "flex" and on what issues? Some things are worth sacrificing a job for yet some things are not. Are you clear about and at peace with what those things are?
3. What are you not willing to compromise on for the sake of keeping your job?
4. Are you able to communicate with your boss about your concerns? Have you equipped yourself with communication

tools to address issues with your boss directly? If not, what is stopping you? Would you be more comfortable with a mediator in a three-way meeting?

5. Review your job description and or contract. Is your career going the way you want it to? If not, what are you going to do about it? Would you be comfortable in discussing changes you might want to make in your career with your boss?

Conclusion

Being a productive and enthusiastic employee makes for better business, better relationships, and less stress all around. The responsibility for creating your positive career is yours alone. Be clear on who you are at work. Learn to communicate your boundaries with respect for yourself and others. Finding where the flexibility is with everyone's boundaries becomes easier when we look at situations from our point of view and then put ourselves in the other person's shoes. Deal with the conflicts as they arise so resentment and anger do not build up. We spend so much of our lives working, so why not make the workplace a positive place to be?

Chapter 8
Global Lines - Crossing Boundaries to Make a Difference

One's life must matter.
Margaret Thatcher

When we get empowered by setting strong boundaries for ourselves, and have faced some challenges with this new understanding, life starts to look different. It becomes easier to see beyond the small circle of our life to reach out and help others. The gratitude I felt from getting a "second chance" at life gave me new strength and the desire to help others get more empowered in their lives. There are endless ways that we can help others less fortunate than ourselves to have a better life, and so many great causes to which we can devote time and energy. Most of us get so caught up in our own day-to-day lives that we look the other way when we see a social problem or issue that urgently needs our attention. It's so much easier to stay in the safety zone of our personal lives than to reach out to help others in need.

In this chapter, I want to tell you a story about an experience that changed my way of seeing things and opened my eyes. Then we'll look at some inspiring examples of people who were willing to step up and cross personal and global boundaries to make a difference in the lives of others.

"The Waiting Room"

Gratitude was not something I felt when I was first diagnosed with breast cancer. I was in great shape, spent my life "eating for health," took anti-cancer supplements and had "zero" risk factors for this disease. So when I was told I had breast cancer I was angry and shocked. As I waited for test results from biopsies and two surgeries, I had time to feel sorry for myself and contemplate my death and my life. Fortunately, the test results showed the cancer had not spread to my lymph nodes, which meant, in my case, that chemotherapy or a mastectomy would not be necessary. What was necessary for me was to embrace this opportunity to re-think my life and fix what was wrong within me and the choices I had made.

I did; however, have radiation treatment and volunteered for the clinic trial related to it. This trial involved going for a dose of radiation twice a day, once first thing in the morning and again at the end of the day, for only five days instead of the usual 16 or more. I was elated to be in this trial. Now I was starting to feel thankful.

When the first day of my treatment came on a Monday morning; I bounced with joy into the cancer clinic, with my MP3 player and a book to pass the time, changed into the ugly blue hospital gown, and sat in the waiting room. About 60 seconds after sitting down, I noticed the woman beside me. Feeling friendly, I struck up a conversation with her. She was in her early 30's, had lost all her hair and nails from chemo treatments, and was undergoing radiation sessions for several months. Her diagnosis was near hopeless and the poor woman's husband had left her and their three children to fend for themselves. I fought back the tears for my "sister," and could not dare utter a word about my journey, as it was trivial by comparison with hers.

Monday afternoon, I returned for my second treatment. Once again, I was feeling grateful and very happy to be alive. When I bounced into the waiting room, it was full of men and women, all bald and pale, some holding vomiting bags, just in case. My cheerful disposition vanished and my heart grew heavy as I witnessed the effects of cancer treatments on these patients. By Wednesday, my third day of radiation treatments, I was more cautious when entering the waiting room. On my fourth day, I felt truly touched and humbled by the stories that people shared with me as we sat together in the waiting room. Every day I felt more grateful for my life – ecstatic to be alive.

Friday morning came, and once more I was feeling alive and "bouncy". As I went to change into that blue hospital gown, I braced myself and peeked around the corner into the waiting room to see who was there. No one! I could continue to be my cheerful self. So off I went to change. Now, it's easy to tell the patients from the support people in the waiting room from their blue gowns. When I came out to sit down, my heart dropped and I felt the pain in my stomach. There were now two people sitting in the room. One was a man who was probably in his late 30's. He was not wearing the hospital gown: his ten-year-old son was. Our eyes met for what seemed a long time and tears were shared. No words were ever spoken that day in the waiting room. The pain and sorrow was too heavy for words.

The next day, I held my ten-year-old son very tightly as I greeted him home from his week away at summer camp. I never again complained about having breast cancer at age 50. My life has been full of dreams that came true, wonderful adventures, and I have two healthy children who have given me the greatest joy.

During my journey back to health, I was in the "waiting room" for a long time. There I had to deal with the pain of recovering from my illness and the pain from still deeper wounds that I was had been trying to cover up. When I got well at last, I decided that it was time to leave the waiting room behind me for good. I wanted to think about what I could contribute to the well being of others and to our beautiful world. I embraced the opportunities in my life as never before. Now it was my time to give back and be of service to others.

Giving Back to Help Others

What is it that causes someone to reach out and lend a hand rather than look the other way?

Sometimes we see an injustice or act of cruelty that crosses our personal boundary and we can no longer turn a blind eye. We stand up and dig in our heels and we set a boundary of intolerance. The people that make a difference in our world are those who are willing to act on it.

Let's look at some of the organizations and that started because people with a mission cared enough to challenge boundaries. To follow are some examples of extraordinary individuals who stepped up to make a difference in our world.

Ecopreneurs with Vision - Connecting Lives with Resources

One man's trash is another man's treasure **– 1-800-GOT- JUNK?**

One of the leading-edge Canadian companies with a mission to make a difference is 1-800-GOT JUNK?. CEO Brian Scudamore has built his innovative recycling business into a 100-plus-million dollar company.

The company website states: "We're the junk removal company that handles the tough stuff - and we ensure that your junk gets recycled, donated or disposed of responsibly… Since 1989, we've saved over 1.5 billion pounds of junk from the landfill and counting." This is clearly a company with a big vision.

Scudamore believes in supporting a work culture that reflects values of strong integrity through communication. Once a day, the employees and management have a "huddle". The purpose is to communicate about what is going on. First, they share the good news in their personal lives and in the business. Then the challenges in the workplace are discussed. Unlike the traditional employer-employee relationship, Scudamore encourages his employees to freely discuss their problems and issues so that everyone can learn from it. An emphasis on honest communication in the workplace fosters understanding and cooperation. This inspiring model could be used to improve any workplace environment. 1-800-GOT-JUNK? was listed as one of the Best Workplaces in Canada, and three years running, among the Best Companies to Work for in BC.

Waste not, want not - Giving Everyone a Fair Share

Activist Tristram Stuart, author of *Waste: Uncovering the Global Food Scandal,* is making a difference in resolving the issue of land usage as well as the human rights issue of starving populations. Stuart has researched into the resources it takes to produce the vast amounts of food put on the market for consumers. His research shows that much of the food produced is completely wasted. "Western countries throw out nearly half of their food, not because it's inedible – but because it doesn't look appealing," says Stuart.

Stuart began his data collecting with "unofficial bin inspections" of the food thrown out by super markets. There he found fresh food that was wasted, such as jars of food that were not opened or broken, and were unexpired. He gathered information about details such as where all the bread crusts go from fresh bread. Of course, we know the answer: into the garbage. Farmers discard tons of fresh, perfectly edible food because it is not the right size and or shape for market. Forty to sixty percent of fish caught at sea are thrown back because they do meet the standards for the fish market. Stuart's research shows that supermarkets throw out huge quantities of food items to meet cosmetic standards. The rich countries waste enormous amounts of food while a billion people are starving.

FareShare, a national United Kingdom charity operating since 2004, has stepped up to help balance the scales and share the wealth of the world's food resources. The organization's mission is to relieve food poverty and reduce food waste. FareShare does this by taking surplus food and drink from the food industry and redistributing it to smaller food charities such as soup kitchens and breakfast clubs. The organization regularly hosts "Feeding the 5,000" events all over the world where discarded fresh food feeds thousands. This is fresh, healthy food, not food in a decaying condition. By taking this perfectly good food and getting it into the mouths of those in need, FareShare shows us an easy solution for feeding the hungry while eliminating food waste.

Stuart points out another positive benefit: "If we wasted less we would buy less. That would leave the food on the world market for internationally traded commodities like wheat and would then be available for people in Africa and Asia who buy food on the same international market as us. So it is in the international market that we are literally taking food out of the mouths of the hungry" (TED TALKS). For Stuart to make this positive change in the world takes not only individuals to volunteer to gather and distribute the actual food, but also people to put pressure on governments to make supportive changes. Stuart has set the boundary to no longer tolerate this situation. He says in his TED talk, "We, the people, do have the power to stop [the] tragic waste of resources if we regard it as socially unacceptable to waste food. Stop trashing our land to grow food that no one eats"

Project HANDS – Reaching out to Help Others

If you witness a fall, shouldn't you put out your hand?
www.projectshands

"The scales of the world are unbalanced. While many live with more than they need, others fight to survive on an unthinkable amount of nothing"
www.projectshands

Project HANDS is a non-profit organization based in Canada

whose mission is to help the indigenous Maya population of South and Central America. The organization's goal is to provide healthcare to people with extremely minimal healthcare in rural regions such as Guatemala. Many of these people had never seen a doctor before Project HANDS volunteers came to help.

The organization also promotes education for children living in impoverished conditions in such areas as Guatemala. Although the recent volunteer effort has primarily focused on helping the Maya population, Project HANDS aims to spread its volunteer effort worldwide and "offer a hand to anyone who reaches for it."

Dr. Matthew Mosher, a specialist in plastic surgery in the Vancouver area, has volunteered to provide reconstructive plastic surgery with Canadian surgical teams on numerous Project HANDS trips to Guatemala. On the first trip, Mosher's team completed 75 procedures on 40 patients in just ten days. Their patients included children with severe burn injuries and congenital deformities, along with old indigenous people with various health issues and injuries.

Dr. Mosher reflects on this trip, "Doing surgery in this rural environment was both challenging and rewarding. Most patients only spoke one of the many Mayan dialects and had to travel by foot and by bus for many hours to get to the surgery clinic. Many of the stories and circumstances associated with these patients were heartbreaking and hard to imagine for those of us so fortunate to live and work in North America. However, despite their poverty, the Guatemalan patients were engaging, joyous and so grateful for our help. This trip really affected me as I thought about my own children and quality of our lives compared to our patients in Guatemala." (www.projecthands.org)

Bearing Witness to Raise Awareness

If people don't see the effects of a social issue or problem firsthand with their very own eyes, they often won't think about it. Most people just carry on with life as usual unless an issue hits close to home and crosses a personal boundary that's intolerable. Sometimes it takes another person to bear witness for us and make it impossible for us to ignore a problem any more. We are fortunate for the authors and documentary filmmakers dedicated to calling injustice to our attention by bringing true stories and images to life. It is mainly by raising awareness of our common humanity that people get inspired to support change in the world.

The fight against poverty in the United States, Canada, and every country in the world is a never-ending battle. Yet there are those who continue the battle to help the poor. Most people would rather keep the issue at arms length maybe give donations and not get close and personal with this painful reality. Yet there are those who are willing to fight the battle to help the poor. Journalist Barbara Ehrenreich tells the story in *Nickel and Dimed: On (Not) Getting By in America* how she faced the issue head on by going underground to do research. Ehrenreich worked at low-level jobs to experience the difficulties of poverty first hand. Her intense, in-depth analysis brought insights to the subject never before considered. This information spread through the media and changed how people view the poor. The stereotype of the poor as lazy people living off the government changed when Ehrenreich showed the true story. Many poor Americans work long hard hours for extremely low pay, often working at two or three jobs to support their families. Barbara Ehrenreich's work is an example of what can be done when we step up to make a positive impact on society by getting the word out in a big way.

Standing Up for Human Rights – Peaceful Resistance

It takes an individual with extraordinary courage and integrity to fight for the cause of human justice. LICADHO (Cambodian League for the Promotion and Defense of Human Rights), the largest human rights organization in Cambodia, was founded by Dr. Kek Galabru. Dr. Kek fled Cambodia during the civil war in the 1980s to live in Canada. She vowed to return to help support the basic rights of her people once peace was restored to her country. It was largely through the efforts of this brave woman that peace efforts were initiated and the peace treaty was signed that ended the war. Based on a philosophy of non-violence, LICADHO initiatives support the rights of women and children, promote education, and address issues such as homelessness from land grabbing in Phnom Penh.

Finding Your Opportunity to Give Back

There are hundreds of causes that scream out to us every day for help, causes that require someone to stand up and draw a boundary that says, "No! I will not put up with that anymore!" To step up and say, "Yes! I want to help" could mean that you have to open up a personal boundary and move beyond your safety zone.

There are four areas where contributions of your time and energy are needed: your family, your local community, your country, and your global community. Your influence as an individual starts close to home, with your smallest circle of family and friends, and moves out from there. It's important to give priority to your personal and professional life, but your contribution is always needed in the wider community.

1. Your Family Unit

Many parents work to support their children while also taking care of the domestic chores at home to provide a healthy environment, and yet make the time to interact with their offspring. Being fully engaged in parenting contributes not only to the family unit, but it also helps to make the world a better place by giving us children who will become solid citizens.

Children need parents to be their advocates for handling

relationships with other children in school or in social activities outside the home. A great example of a situation where parents need to intervene is with bullying. Children need to learn how to say, "No" to bullies. Anyone with a child that has been bullied understands the importance of stepping forward to take action and not allowing this behaviour to continue. Calling attention to the issue helps to expand awareness in the community and then word gets out to the wider public through the media. That's how change happens.

2. Your Local Community

You don't have to look far in any direction to find an opportunity to make an improvement in the lives of others in your community. Donating clothing, giving food donations to your local food bank, or giving some of your time to help fund or build a homeless shelter are just a few of the opportunities in your own backyard.

Brown Bag Mission. Here is the story of how one woman stepped up to make a difference for the homeless people in her community. Joan felt strongly about feeding the hungry on her city's streets. So she started a program to help feed the homeless. All she asked for as donations were brown bag lunches that she distributed once a week at a designated park in the city. Joan could have said, "It's really sad about all those hungry street people" and done nothing about it, because she was too busy and did not have enough money to resolve the problem. Instead, she chose to be creative and do something about a cause she believed in supporting.

Dress for Success. This organization supports a favourite cause of mine. It helps women to get back on their feet and become successful in a career.

Their mission is "to promote the economic independence of disadvantaged women by providing professional attire, a network of support and the career development tools to help women thrive in work and in life" (www.dressforsuccess.org). You can find a branch office for this organization in most major cities if you would like to donate to it.

3. Your Country

Do you want to see changes in your country? What do you feel passionate about? What concerns or interests you? Would you like to become active in politics to support an initiative or policy? Are you interested in drug abuse issues? Military issues? Environmental issues? The fight against child sexual abuse? Do you want to help fund women's shelters? Support legislation for animal rights? Follow your heart to a cause that speaks to you.

4. Your Global Community

Our world needs people to stand up and draw the line in so many areas of our lives. There are literally thousands of causes that you can find to support just by doing a little research. The Internet has given us an amazing opportunity to connect with others, share resources, and support change in our local and global community. Search online to find an organization with a mission and purpose that resonates with you.

Here are some suggestions to get you started:
- Women for Women International www.womenforwomen.org
- Earthwatch www.earthwatch.org
- Habitat for Humanity www.habitat.org
- Zimbabwe Gecko Society. Susan Janetti's project for raising money for widows & orphans. www.zimbabwegecko.com
- Kiva www.kiva.org   Help fund a loan and empower entrepreneurs across the globe.
- International Volunteer Programs Association www.volunteerinternational.org

- Not Just Tourists www.njttoronto.ca
- Travel That Feeds the Soul www.globalvolunteerscanada.ca
- MADD (Mothers Against Drunk Drivers) www.madd.ca

Exploring Your Opportunities for Giving Back

1. Where or in what way do you want to make a difference? What's your motivation?
2. List the causes that you would be willing to participate in to make a difference in the lives of others.
3. Will this participation require you to draw a line(s) in your personal life in order to make it happen? List the ways in which your personal life would be impacted.
4. Why do you want to do this? Why would you like to give your time to a cause?
5. When will you do this? When would you like to begin giving your time to a cause? How will you fit this participation into your schedule?
6. How will you do this? How will you make get started? Who will you contact?

Volunteer Work

There are many exciting opportunities for volunteering at home and abroad. Consider some of the following ways to give your time to a great cause while getting new experience and training.

- An archaeological dig in various countries.
- Trail maintenance in Yellowstone National Park, USA.
- School building in Nicaragua.
- Care for the dying at Mother Teresa's hospice in Calcutta, India.
- Museum restoration in England

Reflection Questions for Volunteering Abroad

To start thinking about volunteer work, consider the following questions:

1. Are you able and willing to work in groups? How do you feel about living and perhaps sharing housing with the volunteer group? Do you have any previous experience that has prepared you to work effectively with others?
2. Are you flexible, open minded, and eager for adventure in an unfamiliar part of the world that is and potentially challenging (physically, emotionally, and psychologically)?
3. Be clear on your interests. What are the main areas that interest you? Which parts of the world are you interested in visiting?
4. Know your needs. What are your requirements as far as food, sleep, accommodations (which can vary greatly) and other needs?
5. Be clear about your reasons for volunteering. Why are you interested in doing volunteer work? Will this experience help you with professional or career goals? Will it give you the opportunity to learn more about a culture?
6. What are your special abilities and strengths? What are your limitations?

Research the organizations in your areas of interest to decide what works best for you. Don't expect the lifestyle and standards of living to be the same as you're accustomed to at home. You will need to be flexible and open minded to adapt to the experience of living in a country where the values and beliefs may be very different from your own. Respect and courtesy go a long way. When it comes to living in foreign countries, do your research to be prepared, but expect the unexpected!

Conclusion

Our world has countless opportunities for you to become a philanthropist if you just open the door to help others. Maybe you don't feel that you were born with a calling to change the world, and maybe you wouldn't want to put your life on the line to help others. But we all can help in our own ways to make a difference. Every act of charity goes out to the whole community. Our world needs whatever you are willing to give. I encourage you to find a cause that truly matters to you and give some of your time, heart, and talent to supporting it.

Living a life that goes against our real selves is time wasted. It means that the soul is diminished and our opportunities for love and greatness are lost. Living with clear intention and giving of yourself enhances all aspects of your life. Don't miss out on the life you really want and die with regret. Be connected with yourself, with others, and with the world.

- Embrace your highest intention.
- Communicate, communicate, communicate.
- Love genuinely.
- Choose to be "known".
- Reach for your highest potential.
- Make choices that enhance your health, not diminish it.
- Be your own best expert.
- Contribute to the happiness of others.
- Stay connected.
- Be a person of honour and integrity.
- Know who you are and set boundaries for success on all fronts!

Biography

Leslie heads her own company, Flawless Delivery - Public Speaking at its Finest, where she facilitates seminars and one-on-one coaching for anyone in need of professional speaking skills, based in Vancouver B.C.

As a keynote speaker and workshop presenter, Leslie shares her passion and commitment to setting strong boundaries with integrity.

In the Toastmaster International organization, she became the provincial champion of "Impromptu Speaking" in 2011. As her own speaking career evolved, she participated in many competitions; from humourous to impromptu; from evaluation to international.

Judging at competitions and evaluating speakers is one of her fortes. In 2008, Leslie served as a judge in the semi-finalists International Speech Contest at the Toastmasters International Conference in Calgary, Alberta. Leslie has devoted many hours of volunteer work within the Toastmasters organization while concurrently working on her business, being a mom, and serving her community.

An outdoor enthusiast, Leslie is an avid cross country skier in the winter months and an enthusiastic hiker and cyclist in the summer months.

Overall, through her commitment to live with intention and integrity, Leslie strives to enhance the lives of others.

If you would like more information on Leslie Fierling

Leslie Fierling DTM Professional Speaker

Speaker Bureau Manager
In Partnership with Vox Presenters
www.voxpresenters.com

Contact Information

Phone: 604-329-5531
Email: leslie@flawlessdeliveryspeaking.com
Website: flawlessdeliveryspeaking.com
(Flawless Delivery is a division of Kinetic Ventures Inc.)

About Flawless Delivery and Leslie Fierling

Flawless Delivery offers today's professionals the tools to augment their communication skills. Leslie's coaching techniques help to develop public speaking skills while enhancing one's unique style. Her personalized feedback sessions are set in a safe environment where her clients feel comfortable to meet their challenges.

Services

Speaking Engagements

Leslie offers a variety of presentations, seminars, and keynote speeches on the subject of, "Boundary Setting for Success".

Coaching

Leslie coaches with an intent to bring speakers to their highest level of professionalism. She emphasizes using both accredited techniques and heartfelt emotion to communicate their messages with conviction.

Evaluation & Feedback

Leslie offers a formal evaluation after attending and videotaping your live speaking event.

Workshops

Boundary Setting for Success

Benefits:
- Regain control of your work life: whether you are an employer or employee.
- Develop and maintain self-respect.
- Be authentic.
- Find fulfillment in your personal and professional life.

Topics:
1. B & B: Business and Boundaries: As a leader, do you erode the boundaries of your team members or do they erode yours?
   - Understand the difference between compromise and settling.
   - Learn to set clear, strong boundaries with respect.
   - Build a team of positive and purposeful individuals.

2. Global Lines: Crossing boundaries to make a difference
3. Experts: When are you giving your power away?
4. Love Lines: A game plan for relationships.
5. Keep the Drive Alive: Intimate Connections, Raise the blinds and draw the lines.

Public Speaking

The "How To" of Public Speaking

Workshops are available to speakers with any level of experience.

Testimonials

Leslie Fierling is an excellent public speaker. She speaks with confidence, clarity, and great expression. She has a passion for her subject and this allows her to connect easily with her audience. Leslie holds the highest designation in Toastmasters International as a Distinguished Toastmaster (DTM). It took her three years to accomplish this feat and it involved her becoming proficient in all facets of public speaking. Leslie is professional and can always can be relied on to provide presentations of the very highest quality.
Alan Warburton - DTM

Leslie's professional speaking skills draws in her audience whether she is speaking from the heart or presenting educational material. When she puts out a call for action one feels compelled to become involved. She has a way of gripping the attention of the listener, which leaves her audience fulfilled, educated, moved or entertained… she's really good!
Sandy VanDeKinder - Past President of Early Edition Toastmasters - Dog Trainer

I would recommend Leslie to any organization looking for a speaker… Whatever the topic, she is clearly disciplined in her approach and gets the message across in a very inspirational way…Being a fellow Toastmaster and having heard many of her speeches, I always looked forward to her presentations and her power to influence. Very enjoyable speaker.
Susan Young, Owner, YoungPro Promotions Products

Leslie is an expert with public speaking. She is empowering to work with. She puts her entire being into everything she does. There is no "half way" with Leslie. She inspires me to be more than I thought I could be with my speaking. Always true to her word, I would recommend working with her the next time you are looking for a speaking coach.
Christine Till (LIONESS) The Marketing Mentress

Leslie is an enthusiastic, dynamic and seasoned public speaker and Toastmaster. I've known Leslie for many years and competed with her in District Provincial Competitions. Leslie is comfortable speaking before an audience of 25 or 300 and has a passion for her message. Always determined to deliver a message that the audience will not forget, Leslie is a remarkable orator and raconteur. I highly endorse Leslie to any event planner, convention organizer or Toastmaster.
Reg Boaler, President, Boaler Glasswasher Inc.

If you want to get on the path to be a published author by **Influence Publishing** please go to **www.InspireABook.com**

More information on our other titles and how to submit your own proposal can be found at **www.InfluencePublishing.com**

CPSIA information can be obtained at www.ICGtesting.com
Printed in the USA
LVOW04s2233220814

400477LV00011B/202/P